The Dinosaur
Dictionary

THE DINOSAUR

By Donald F. Glut

Introductions by ALFRED SHERWOOD ROMER
*Museum of Comparative Zoology,
Harvard University*

and DAVID TECHTER
Rochester Museum and Science Center

DICTIONARY

BONANZA BOOKS
New York

To

Dr. Edwin H. Colbert,

former Curator of Vertebrate Paleontology
at the American Museum of Natural History
and currently Curator of Vertebrate Paleontology
at the Museum of Northern Arizona . . .

Alfred Sherwood Romer

former Professor of Zoology at Harvard University
and past Director of that institution's
Museum of Comparative Zoology . . .

. . . for their invaluable help through books and personal letters.

Especially to

David Techter,

former Assistant Preparator of Fossil Vertebrates
at the Field Museum of Natural History
and former Curator of Natural Sciences
at the Rochester Museum and Science Center,

for his years of help and personal guidance.

Copyright © MCMLXXII by Donald F. Glut
All rights reserved.

This 1984 edition is published by Bonanza Books,
distributed by Crown Publishers, Inc.
225 Park Avenue South
New York, New York 10003,
by arrangement with Lyle Stuart, Inc.

Manufactured in the United States of America

Library of Congress Cataloging in Publication Data

Glut, Donald F.
The dinosaur dictionary.

Bibliography: p.
1. Dinosaurs—Dictionaries.   I. Title.
QE862.D5G65   1984   567.9'1'0321   84-18564

ISBN: 0-517 455897

m   l   k   j   i   h

Contents

ACKNOWLEDGMENTS

Sincere thanks are due the following, both living and deceased, who either directly or indirectly contributed to this volume and to the field of paleontology:

Othenio Abel, Roy Chapman Andrews, Joseph Augusta, Barnum Brown, Dean William Buckland, Zdenek Burian, Edward Drinker Cope, Georges Cuvier, Orville Gilpin, Waterhouse Hawkins, Edward Hitchcock, Friedrich von Huene, Werner Janesch, Charles R. Knight, Lawrence Lambe, Gideon Mantell, Henry Fairfield Osborn, Richard Owen, Neave Parker, Charles S. Sternberg, Rudolph F. Zallinger, and Rainer Zangerl.

Also thanks to: Forrest J Ackerman, Larry M. Byrd, Jim Danforth, L. Sprague de Camp, J. L. Dunning, Jim Harmon, Ray Harryhausen, Larry Ivie, Helen B. Jones, Allen G. Kracalik, Roy G. Krenkel, Joe Kubert, David M. Massaro, Helen J. McGinnis, Willis O'Brien, Mary Jean Odano, Winifred Reinders, D. Scott Rogo, Martin Sara, Tom Scherman, Edward Schneider, Gordon Thomas, and Robert W. Wilson.

Special thanks to Julia Glut, my mother, for her tolerance and endurance. When I was a child she took me to Dinosaur Park in Rapid City, South Dakota, and read many books while I looked with a great sense of wonder at the paleontology exhibits in the museums of the United States.

My deepest apologies to anyone I may have neglected to mention.

In every possible example I have attempted to credit illustrations and secure permission for their reproduction. Restorations without credit lines are by the author and based upon skeletons or older restorations.

The following institutions have been more than cooperative in supplying me with data and illustrative material:

The Academy of Natural Sciences of Philadelphia; The Ackerman Archives (which supplied all still photographs taken from motion pictures); American Museum of Natural History, New York; British Museum (Natural History), London; Carnegie Museum, Pittsburgh; Dinosaur National Monument; Los Angeles County Museum of Natural History; Museum of Comparative Zoology, Harvard University, Cambridge, Massachusetts; Peabody Museum of Natural History, Yale University, New Haven, Connecticut; School of Mines and Technology, Rapid City, South Dakota; Sinclair Oil Corporation; United States National Museum, Smithsonian Institution, Washington, D. C.; University of Southern California; and Warner Brothers.

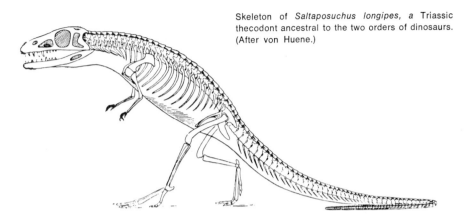

Skeleton of *Saltaposuchus longipes,* a Triassic thecodont ancestral to the two orders of dinosaurs. (After von Huene.)

Introduction 1

In most cases, knowledge of the names of fossil animals is restricted to a small number of scientists.

Not so with dinosaurs. They have attracted the interest of a large section of the public, and study of them has trickled downward through educational channels to become, in many a case, part of the curriculum of early grades. (I remember how startled I was, a number of years ago, to have my nine-year-old son come home from school and talk learnedly about "double-beam"—otherwise *Diplodocus.*)

For the student of dinosaurs there are not only the more technical (and dreary) accounts for the specialists, but also good general accounts on. a less technical level by Colbert and Swinton.

Mr. Glut's book attacks the problem from a different angle, not giving a connected account of dinosaur evolution, but a "dictionary" type of treatment—a work to which the reader can go and immediately find an account (illustrated) of any genus that has attracted his attention. The present volume will, I am sure, prove to be a useful addition to the library of anyone interested in these spectacular former inhabitants of our planet.

ALFRED SHERWOOD ROMER
Former Director
Museum of Comparative Zoology
Harvard University

1

Skeletons of the classic saurischian *Antrodemus (Allosaurus) valens* (left) and ornithischian, *Camptosaurus* (right), realistically mounted in the pose of battle. Courtesy of the Los Angeles County Museum of Natural History.

Introduction 2

There is no denying the popular interest in dinosaurs. Millions have beheld the image of these extinct reptiles on service station signs, on television, at World's Fairs, or at Disneyland, and countless youngsters have admired their mounted skeletons in the nation's museums. I have known a four-year-old who could spout off *Stegosaurus* and *Triceratops* before she could identify a tiger or elephant. Everyone loves dinosaurs.

Yet, when I undertook formal studies in vertebrate paleontology, I was struck by the contrast between popular enthusiasm and scientific knowledge. Everyone knows *Brontosaurus*. Yet how many realize that no skeleton of this beast has ever been found with the skull attached? Even his correct name is in dispute. It seems clear that *Brontosaurus* is the same as the earlier-named *Apatosaurus*, which by the rules has "priority" and should be the proper name. The impressive *Tyrannosaurus* is a household word, yet his somewhat smaller cousin *Gorgosaurus* is known from many more specimens.

In part, popular concepts can be traced back to painter Charles R. Knight, whose vivid murals grace the walls of Chicago's Field Museum and the American Museum of Natural History in New York. Hardly any dinosaur not portrayed by Knight has ever become known to the layman.

It was just this gap between popular and scientific knowledge that inspired

2

Donald Glut to compile this volume. As a young student he was frustrated by
the difficulty in finding information on some of the less popular ancient reptiles.
There should be a book, he complained, that told about *all* the dinosaurs. Since
none existed, he decided to write the volume himself. After years of research,
here it is, a reference volume for both the scholar and the public.

DAVID TECHTER
Former Curator of Natural Sciences
Rochester Museum and Science Center

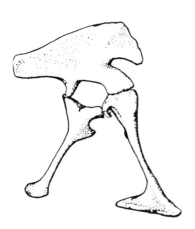 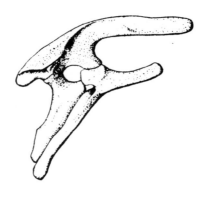

(Left) Pelvis of a typical saurischian dinosaur,
Allosaurus. (Right) Pelvis of the ornithischian
Stegosaurus. (After Gilmore, Romer.)

Courtesy of the Dinosaur Nature Association.

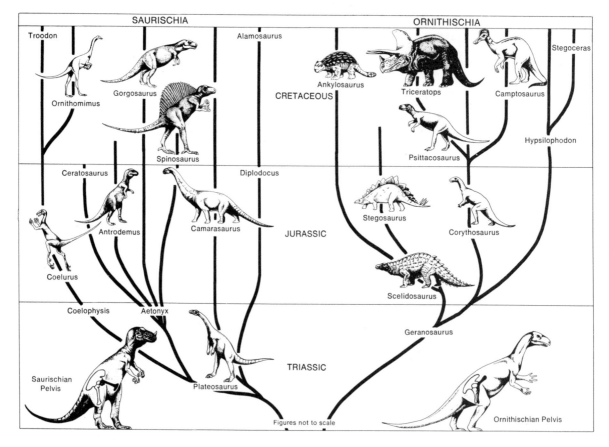

SAURISCHIA

ORNITHISCHIA

Troodon

Alamosaurus

Stegoceras

Ornithomimus

Gorgosaurus

Ankylosaurus

Triceratops

Camptosaurus

CRETACEOUS

Spinosaurus

Psittacosaurus

Hypsilophodon

Ceratosaurus

Diplodocus

Stegosaurus

Corythosaurus

Antrodemus

Camarasaurus

JURASSIC

Coelurus

Scelidosaurus

Coelophysis

Aetonyx

Geranosaurus

Saurischian
Pelvis

TRIASSIC

Plateosaurus

Figures not to scale

Ornithischian Pelvis

A Background

The dinosaurs were the most successful animals ever to walk this planet. For approximately 120 million years, these creatures, which ranged from the size of a chicken to the largest land animals of all time, dominated the earth. Their peculiar forms and the tremendous sizes some of the dinosaurs attained have made them objects of particular fascination.

This book is a dictionary of dinosaurs. It is an alphabetical listing with capsule data of virtually every *genus* of dinosaur known to paleontologists at this time.

We are almost exclusively concerned with genera. Many genera of dinosaurs have numerous species, the differences of which are mostly important to the professional paleontologist who has studied populations of these extinct reptiles. The genus *Triceratops* alone is known from no less than fifteen species (skulls, skeletons, and fragmentary material), the differences being sometimes slight, perhaps nonexistent, or possibly even pathological. Species will be noted when important to distinguish a particular genus and will be shown in many of the illustrations.

This book does not attempt to trace in detail the evolution of the dinosaurs from their original stock; nor does it speculate upon the reasons for their extinction or give them any particular significance in the scale of life. Such books have already been written—and rewritten. Most of them are valuable. For these particular insights, I encourage you to read the books cited in the bibliography.

The Dinosaur Dictionary is a reference book, a supplement presenting the most complete and up-to-date catalogue of dinosaurs.

Naturally, a project such as this has presented problems. Paleontology is a highly speculative and opinionated science. This is primarily true in the case of fossil fragments. Experts in the field use their own judgments in classifying various incomplete skulls and skeletons, so that no one has yet been able to define every genus of dinosaur exclusively.

Courtesy of the Dinosaur Nature Association.

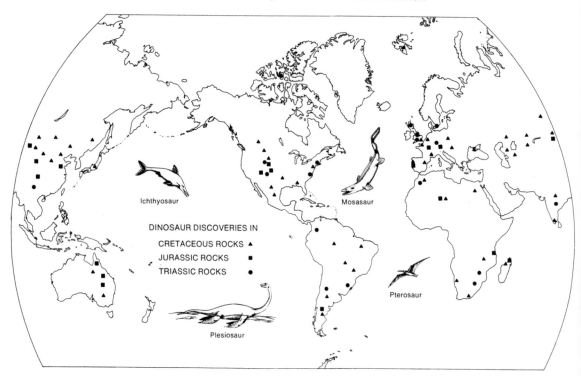

Ichthyosaur

Mosasaur

DINOSAUR DISCOVERIES IN

CRETACEOUS ROCKS ▲
JURASSIC ROCKS ■
TRIASSIC ROCKS ●

Pterosaur

Plesiosaur

For example, returning to the horned dinosaur *Triceratops,* Dr. Edwin H. Colbert will say that the genus is not the same as *Agathaumas* and *Sterrholophus.* On the other hand, Professor Alfred Sherwood Romer regards them as synonymous. Both men are experts. In such cases, I have listed them as individual genera, indicating that they might possibly be identical.

It is impossible to present a restoration of every genus of dinosaur. Since many of these are known through incomplete skeletons, or more unfortunately, fragments, some varieties are impossible to restore. Many genera have never been restored, since they might closely resemble other types of dinosaurs. Therefore, when looking up *Aepisaurus* in this dictionary to find that "this genus is extremely similar to *Titanosaurus,*" the next step would be to refer to the latter entry.

As already stated, this book is not intended to give a comprehensive history of the dinosaurs, since such information can be acquired in other texts. However, before presenting the list of genera it would be significant to give at least a brief and skeletal background description of the nature of these extinct animals.

The dinosaurs were reptiles that reigned over the surface of the earth for that 120-million year period known as the Mesozoic Era and generally referred to as the Age of Reptiles. This era can be broken down into three distinct periods—the Triassic Period (225 to 180 million years ago), the Jurassic Period (180 to 135 million years ago), and the Cretaceous Period (135 to 70 million years ago).

Dinosaurs first appeared in the latter portion of the Triassic Period. By the Jurassic Period, certain of these creatures reached gargantuan proportions. By the culmination of the Cretaceous Period, these erstwhile rulers of the entire planet were extinct.

We have been using the term *dinosaur* quite liberally. This deserves some explanation since the word *dinosaur,* though commonly used, is in truth a misnomer. In the nineteenth century, when the first dinosaur fossils were discovered, Sir Richard Owen, a paleontologist and anatomist, created the word *Dinosauria* to represent all of these remains. The term combined the Greek word *deinos,* meaning "terrible," and *sauros,* meaning "lizard." Surely, he thought, all these creatures must have been terrible when they lumbered over the earth. The term *Dinosauria,* then, implied that all of these creaures belonged to a single biological order. Owen was wrong about this, but his error has remained until the present in popular thinking.

Actually, there are two orders of dinosaurs, *Saurischia* and *Ornithischia*—as different from each other as they are from the *Pterosauria* (flying reptiles), *Crocodilia* (alligators and crocodiles), and the ancestors of all four orders, the *Thecodontia.*

We should here state that the two orders of dinosaurs fall into two subdivisions under the great class *Reptilia.* This general classification of reptiles may further be broken down into the subclass *Diapsida* (skulls have lower and upper holes behind the eyes), and then into the suborder *Archosauria,* or "ruling reptiles." The dinosaurs, pterosaurs, crocodilians, and thecodonts are all archosaurs. The thecodonts appeared in the early Triassic Period and were characterized by strong hindlegs and smaller forelimbs. Their skulls were deep and narrow and looked very much like the earliest types of dinosaurs. From the order *Thecodontia* evolved the two great orders of dinosaurs, *Saurischia* and *Ornithischia.*

Saurischia is the order of "lizard-hipped" dinosaurs, as derived from the Greek, because of the typically reptilian structure of the pelvis. The top bone of the pelvis, the *ilium,* connects with the vertebrae. Protruding from this bone is the *pubis,* while a third bone, the *ischium,* extends downward from the *ilium* and behind the *pubis. Ornithischia,* the order of "bird-hipped" dinosaurs, implies that the pelvis resembles that of the birds. The *ilium* is considerably elongated, while the *pubis* is parallel to the *ischium.*

There are other differences in the two orders.

Teeth appear along the front and side margins of the jaws, or only in the front, in the saurischian skull. To the contrary, teeth are always absent from the front of the ornithischian jaws. In some ornithischian forms, the mouth ends in a horny, birdlike beak. Also, the saurischian skull is equipped with openings before the eye to subtract some of the animal's mass. Behind the eyes are two large holes that housed the jaw muscles of the creature. In the ornithischian skull, these openings have been considerably reduced or even eliminated.

Only in *Saurischia* did carnivorous forms exist, while only in *Ornithischia* were there armored varieties.

Of the two orders, *Saurischia* was the most enduring. The order emerged in the Triassic Period and flourished until the end of the Mesozoic Era. Ornithischians did not appear until the Triassic Period had passed and did not attain greatest success until Cretaceous times.

For the sake of simplicity in identifying and understanding the hundreds of genera listed in this book it is imperative that I present the following breakdown of the two orders. This will have more meaning when, for example, a genus is described as "a megalosaur," which can be further clarified by referral to this breakdown. Thus, much repetition is eliminated.

The two orders, *Saurischia* and *Ornithischia,* may be subdivided as follows:

Order *Saurischia*

**Suborder *Theropoda*—almost exclusively carnivorous; bipedal, with strong hind legs and small forelimbs with claws used primarily for grasping; flourished during the entire Mesozoic Era.

Infraorder *Coelurosauria*—small theropods, somewhat birdlike; the bones hollow, their small heads at the end of rather long necks; flourished throughout Mesozoic Era.

Families:

Ammosauridae—uncertain theropod genera.

Hallopodidae—long and flexible neck; short ischium; femur shorter than tibia; metatarsals long, slender; forelimbs equipped with three functional digits; flourished during the Upper Jurassic.

Podokesauridae—small; primitive; built for hopping; neck relatively short; forelimbs very short and slender, with five digits; hind legs very long; three or four metatarsals; flourished during the Triassic.

Segisauridae—similar to *Hallopodidae* and *Coeluridae;* characterized by the persistence of the collar bone; body vertebrae and long body bones solid; resembled thecodonts; flourished during Upper Triassic and Lower Jurassic.

Coeluridae—very small, light, with hollow bones; front legs long and slender; femur larger than tibia; flourished during Upper Jurassic and Lower Cretaceous.

Ornithomimidae—very light; of average height; not hunters; skull very small, with slender, toothless jaws; long forelimbs with three digits; femur shorter than tibia; long feet with three close digits resembling those of the ostrich; built for running; flourished during the Upper Cretaceous.

Infraorder *Carnosauria*—large theropods, with great skulls and short necks; massive bones, hind feet birdlike; small to tiny forelimbs; flourished throughout the Mesozoic.

Families:

Palaeosauridae—heavy; strong claws; flourished during Upper Triassic.

Teratosauridae—early forms, but already showing signs of the giant carnosaurs to come; teeth with two sharp edges, the points turning back, and all laterally compressed, suitable for tearing flesh; forelimbs very short, armed with three curved claws; feet with three digits, the second, third, and fourth all functional; the fifth digit present but reduced and nonfunctional; already specialized as giant hunters; especially successful in Germany and South Africa; flourished during the Triassic.

The ceratopsian dinosaur *Monoclonius nasicornis* stands beside a nest of its eggs.

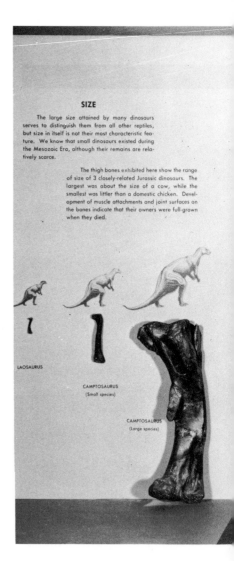

SIZE

The large size attained by many dinosaurs serves to distinguish them from all other reptiles, but size in itself is not their most characteristic feature. We know that small dinosaurs existed during the Mesozoic Era, although their remains are relatively scarce.

The thigh bones exhibited here show the range of size of 3 closely-related Jurassic dinosaurs. The largest was about the size of a cow, while the smallest was littler than a domestic chicken. Development of muscle attachments and joint surfaces on the bones indicate that their owners were full-grown when they died.

LAOSAURUS

CAMPTOSAURUS
(Small species)

CAMPTOSAURUS
(Large species)

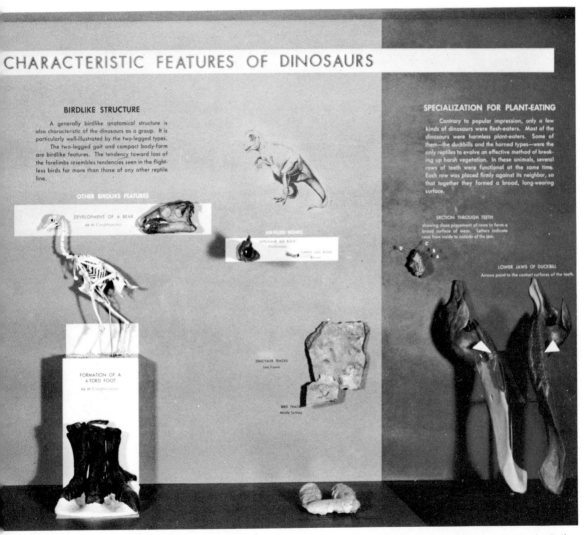

CHARACTERISTIC FEATURES OF DINOSAURS

BIRDLIKE STRUCTURE

A generally birdlike anatomical structure is also characteristic of the dinosaurs as a group. It is particularly well-illustrated by the two-legged types.

The two-legged gait and compact body-form are birdlike features. The tendency toward loss of the forelimbs resembles tendencies seen in the flightless birds far more than those of any other reptile line.

OTHER BIRDLIKE FEATURES

DEVELOPMENT OF A BEAK

AIR-FILLED BONES

DINOSAUR LEG BONE

TURKEY LEG BONE

FORMATION OF A 4-TOED FOOT

DINOSAUR TRACKS

BIRD TRACKS

SPECIALIZATION FOR PLANT-EATING

Contrary to popular impression, only a few kinds of dinosaurs were flesh-eaters. Most of the dinosaurs were harmless plant-eaters. Some of them—the duckbills and the horned types—were the only reptiles to evolve an effective method of breaking up harsh vegetation. In these animals, several rows of teeth were functional at the same time. Each row was placed firmly against its neighbor, so that together they formed a broad, long-wearing surface.

SECTION THROUGH TEETH

showing close placement of rows to form a broad surface of wear. Letters indicate rows from inside to outside of the jaw.

LOWER JAWS OF DUCKBILL

Arrows point to the contact surfaces of the teeth.

Courtesy of the Smithsonian Institution.

Megalosauridae—a large family of theropods; skull large with long jaws; teeth typically carnosaurian, double edges usually rounded; forelimbs very short; hind legs powerful and adapted for running; femur longer than tibia; claws large and sharp, curved for tearing; flourished from Lower Jurassic into Cretaceous times.

Tyrannosauridae—with the general characteristics of the megalosaurs, but larger and more powerful; forelimbs reduced to virtual uselessness; high specialization and great bulk may have forced some genera to become scavengers; flourished in Upper Cretaceous.

Infraorder *Prosauropoda*—ancestors of sauropods; both small and large varieties; carnivorous, herbivorous, and omnivorous forms; skull small with teeth shaped like leaves; bones heavy; stocky hind limbs; flourished during Triassic.

Families:
Thecodontosauridae—extremely primitive; resembled thecodonts; flourished during Middle and Upper Triassic.
Plateosauridae—heavy and large; flourished during Middle and Upper Triassic.

Plateosauridae—heavy and large; flourished during Middle and upper Triassic.

Melanorosauridae—trend toward quadrupedal locomotion; flourished primarily during Upper Triassic, with some representation in Middle Triassic.

Suborder *Sauropoda*—usually gigantic, quadrupedal forms, with heavy bones; small head at end of long neck; long tail; broad feet; flourished from Jurassic through Cretaceous.

Families:
Brachiosauridae—forelimbs may be as long as or even longer than hind legs; four sacral vertebrae; flourished from Middle Jurassic to Lower Cretaceous.

Titanosauridae—forelimbs shorter than hind legs; flourished from Middle Jurassic through Upper Cretaceous.

Order *Ornithischia*—all were herbivorous.

Suborder *Ornithopoda*—both bipedal and semi-quadrupedal forms.

Families:
Hypsilophodontidae—generally small; feet clawed; flourished during both Jurassic and Cretaceous.

The suborder *Stegosauria* is exemplified by the plated dinosaur *Stegosaurus stenops*. Model by C. W. Gilmore. Courtesy of the Smithsonian Institution.

A prehistoric conflict is about to take place between the peaceful, long-necked *Brontosaurus (Apatosaurus)* and the flesh-eating *Allosaurus*. A scene from *The Animal World,* a Warner Bros. motion picture of 1955.

The gigantic sauropod *Brontosaurus (Apatosaurus)* feeding on some Jurassic vegetation. The creature was given life on the motion picture screen through the stop-motion special effects of Willis O'Brien and Ray Harryhausen in Warner Bros.' *The Animal World* (1955).

Iguanodontidae—all sizes; limbs massive; flourished during Jurassic and Cretaceous.

Hadrosauridae—all large; "duck-bills" formed by flat, broad jaws; air storage and/or olfactory-aiding crests sometimes adorning the skulls; new teeth replaced those worn-out; adapted for swimming; flourished exclusively during Cretaceous.

Pachycephalosauridae—"bone-headed" dinosaurs, so named because of domed skull; various sizes; probably entirely terrestrial; flourished only during Cretaceous.

Suborder *Stegosauria*—quadrupedal, with forelimbs shorter than hind legs; protected by armor plating and/or spikes; flourished during Jurassic through Lower Cretaceous.

Styracosaurus (left) vs. *Allosaurus* (right) in a battle to the death only possible on the motion picture screen. A scene from Warner Bros.' science fiction film *The Valley of Gwangi* (1969).

Families:
Scelidosauridae—primitive stegosaurs; appeared as modified versions of later stegosaurs.

Stegosauridae—more advanced forms; two rows of upstanding armor plating and spikes; flourished from Jurassic through Lower Cretaceous.

Suborder *Ankylosauria*—stocky armored dinosaurs; short, broad feet; bony armor covering body and sometimes the head; tail sometimes armed with spikes and/or climaxed with a heavy club; head carried low; flourished only during Cretaceous.

Families:
Acanthopholidae—primitive forms, hinting that early ankylosaurs may have evolved from the stegosaurs; flourished all throughout Cretaceous.

This life-size statue of *Triceratops* was equipped with a moving head. The creature was one of the "Dinoland" exhibits at the New York World's Fair (1964-65). Courtesy of the Sinclair Oil Corporation.

One *Triceratops* eyes another in this scene from the First National (Warner Bros.) silent film classic of 1925, *The Lost World*, based on the novel by Sir Arthur Conan Doyle.

Nodosauridae—skull covered with a number of armored plates; lateral temporal openings covered with hard bones; temporal nostrils; teeth small; entire body covered with bony armor; flourished all throughout Cretaceous.

Suborder *Ceratopsia*—variations in size; skulls large or gigantic, sometimes accompanied by horns; snout beak-like; almost exclusively quadrupedal; flourished during Upper Cretaceous.

Families:

Psittacosauridae*—ancestral; bipedal, with rather large forelimbs; small size.

Protoceratopsidae—primitive; hornless, with or without frill; small size; quadrupedal only.

Ceratopsidae—large to giant forms; frilled skull enormous; horns of different sizes; quadrupedal.

Pachyrhinosauridae—same as above, with coarse boss covering the top of the snout.

Restoration of the armored dinosaur *Ankylosaurus* by Neave Parker. Such protection evolved by the slower moving herbivorous dinosaurs probably forced the largest flesh-eaters to become scavengers.

---

* Considered by some paleontologists to be a family under the suborder *Ornithopoda*.

Actual-size statue of the great carnivore *Tyrannosaurus* at the New York World's Fair (1964-65). The model was equipped with a moving lower jaw. Courtesy of the Sinclair Oil Corporation.

Tracks left by a theropod dinosaur in sandstone. Courtesy of the
Field Museum of Natural History.

The giant *Brontosaurus (Apatosaurus)* as it appeared at the New York World's Fair (1964-65).
Courtesy of the Sinclair Oil Corporation.

The crested hadrosaur *Corythosaurus* as represented by this life-size model at "Dino-land" at the New York World's Fair (1964-65). Courtesy of the Sinclair Oil Corporation.

Broken dinosaur egg discovered in the Gobi Desert of Mongolia. Courtesy of the Field Museum of Natural History.

Abbreviations

In order to simplify the text following each genus of dinosaur, and to prevent the space-consuming repetition of such frequently occurring terms as "Theropoda" and "Jurassic," the following abbreviations shall be used:

Suborders—Ank., Ankylosauria; Cer., Ceratopsia; Orn., Ornithopoda; Saur., Sauropoda; Steg., Stegosauria; and Ther., Theropoda.

Families—Acanth., Acanthopholidae; Ammo., Ammosauridae; Brach., Brachiosauridae; Cerat., Ceratopsidae; Coel., Coeluridae; Had., Hadrosauridae; Hall., Hallopodidae; Hyps., Hypsilophodontidae; Iguan., Iguanodontidae; Meg., Megalosauridae; Mel., Melanosauridae; Nod., Nodosauridae; Ornith., Ornithomimidae; Pachy., Pachycephalosauridae; Pachyrhin., Pachyrhinosauridae; Palae., Palaeosauridae; Plat., Plateosauridae; Pod., Podokesauridae; Pro., Protoceratopsidae; Psitt., Psittacosauridae; Seg., Segisauridae; Stego., Stegosauridae; Ter., Teratosauridae; Theco., Thecodontosauridae; Titan., Titanosauridae; Tyrann., Tyrannosauridae.

Mesozoic Periods—Trias., Triassic; Jur. Jurassic; Cret., Cretaceous; also, L., Lower; M., Middle; and U., Upper.

The Dinosaur
Dictionary

Restoration of the armored dinosaur *Acanthopholis* by Neave Parker. Courtesy of the British Museum (Natural History).

Restoration of the meat-eating dinosaur *Acrocanthosaurus.*

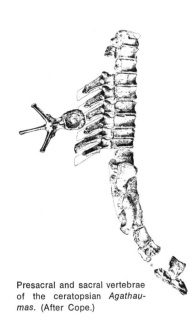

Presacral and sacral vertebrae of the ceratopsian *Agathaumas.* (After Cope.)

A

AACHENOSAURUS—The term was given in 1888 to what was believed to be two hadrosaurian fragments. Later that year the specimens were proved to be pieces of petrified wood.

ABALONIA—(*See* CLADEIODON.)

ACANTHOPHOLIS—*Ank., Acanth., L. and U. Cret.* Known from scattered fossil fragments, this primitive armored dinosaur, from the Chalk Marl of Folkestone and from the Cambridge Greensand in England, apparently had a slender body, armed with spines on the shoulders, and with hard plates.

ACROCANTHOSAURUS—*Ther., Meg., L. Cret.* This giant carnosaur, discovered in Oklahoma, was somewhat related to *Spinosaurus,* although it lacked the extraordinary back spines. The vertebral spines, however, were still considerably high. The head was proportionately smaller than that of theropods of the *Gorgosaurus* variety.

AEGYPTOSAURUS—*Saur., Titan., U. Cret.* From the Baharija of Egypt, this dinosaur is known only from fragments.

AEPISAURUS—*Saur., Titan., L. Cret.* From Europe, this genus is extremely similar to *Titanosaurus.*

AEPOSAURUS—*Ther., U. Trias. or' L. Jur.* Discovered in Asia, fragmentary specimens classify this genus as apparently a theropod.

AETONYX—*Ther., Theco., U. Trias.* This prosauropod from the Stormberg Beds of South Africa is extremely similar to *Thecodontosaurus.*

AGATHAUMAS—*Cer., Cerat., U. Cret.* The name *Agathaumas* has been given to an incomplete skeleton lacking the skull, from Wyoming, and fragmentary material from Colorado. Opinions differ as to whether or not this constitutes a distinct genus or is synonymous with *Triceratops.* One species A. *mortuarius,* known by fragments discovered in Colorado, has also been named *Polyonax.* (*See* POLYONAX, TRICERATOPS.)

AGGIOSAURUS—(*See* MEGALOSAURUS.)

AGROSAURUS—*Ther., Coel., M. and U. Jur.* This genus, discovered on the northeastern coast of Australia, is known only from one tooth, one claw, one segment of a limb, and one tibia almost 8 inches long.

ALAMOSAURUS—*Saur., Titan., U. Cret.* From New Mexico, this genus is quite similar to *Titanosaurus.*

ALBERTOSAURUS—*Ther., Tyrann., U. Cret.* Found in North America, this carnosaur is known primarily from a dentary filled with sharp teeth.

ALBISAURUS—*Orn., Iguan., L. Cret.* The genus was first known through an incomplete tarsal, apparently belonging to an iguanodont dinosaur discovered in Bohemia in 1893 and given the name *Iguanodon? albinus.* A femur over two feet three inches long, nearly complete, discovered in Arizona, was attributed to *Albisaurus* in 1964.

ALECTROSAURUS—*Ther., Tyrann., U. Cret.* The genus, discovered in East Asia, was a large carnosaur. It is known from imperfect skeletal remains indicating that the animal was relatively slender.

ALGOASAURUS—*Saur., Titan., L. Cret.* From South Africa, this dinosaur is known through imperfect skeletal remains. The scapula is similar to that in *Apatosaurus.* The femur, probably over one and one-half feet long when complete, resembles that in *Diplodocus;* the vertebrae, about one and one-half feet high when complete, also resembles those of *Diplodocus.* The tail was less developed than in most sauropods.

ALLOSAURUS—*Ther., Meg., M. and L. Jur. (Antrodemus, Saurophagus; possibly Ceratosaurus, Creosaurus, Dryptosaurus, Labrosaurus, Laelaps, Poecilopleuron.)* This North American carnosaur was the most dangerous predator of the Jurassic Period. As in all carno-

Restoration of *Albertosaurus,* a flesh-eater closely related to *Gorgosaurus,* by Neave Parker. Copyright the *Illustrated London News.*

Incomplete femur of the sauropod *Algoasaurus bauri.* (After Broom.)

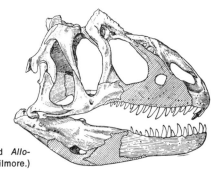

Skull of the theropod *Allosaurus fragilis.* (After Gilmore.)

saurs, its neck was strong but relatively short. Its fore-limbs and hind legs terminated with hands and feet equipped with sharp claws that were efficiently used to pin down, tear, and gash its prey. Powerful leg muscles enabled this hunter to spring at its victims with considerable leaps. The animal attained a length of approximately thirty feet. (*See* CERATOSAURUS, CREO-SAURUS, DRYPTOSAURUS, LABROSAURUS, POECILOPLEURON, SAUROPHAGUS.)

ALTISPINAX—*Ther., Meg., L. Cret.* In this European carnosaur, the neural spines of the dorsal vertebrae

is very high, equal to four times the length of the vertebrae centra. These spines, however, are still not of the proportions of those of *Spinosaurus*.

AMMOSAURUS—*Ther., Coel., U. Trias.* From Connecticut, this dinosaur is quite similar to *Anchisaurus*, except that the tarsus in the foot of the former is more complete than in the latter. The reptile was possibly capable of some quadrupedal locomotion. *Ammosaurus* are related to *Thecodontosaurus* and *Massospondylus,* with bones similar to those of *Zanclodon.*

Stegosaurus prepares to use its spiked tail as a hungry *Allosaurus* stalks toward it, in a diorama of the Jurassic Period. Courtesy of the Milwaukee Public Museum.

Footprints of *Ammopus.* (After Marsh.)

Outlined skeleton of *Ammosaurus major.* (After von Huene.)

The sauropod dinosaur *Amphicoelias altus.* (Modified after an early restoration.)

Skull of *Anatosaurus saskatchewanesis.* Courtesy of the Geological Survey of Canada.

AMPHICOELIAS—*Saur., Titan., M. and U. Jur.* Similar to *Camarasaurus,* this genus was discovered in Colorado.

AMPHISAURUS—(*See* YALEOSAURUS.)

AMYGDALODON—*Saur., Brach., L. Jur.* This genus was discovered in South America.

ANATOSAURUS—*Orn., Had., U. Cret.* (*At least one species of Claosaurus; possibly Diclonius or Thespesius; probably Trachodon.*) This huge ornithopod is the classic "duck-billed dinosaur," so named for the long and low, narrow skull resembling a duck's bill, and for the webbed, three-toed feet. The animal had approximately two thousand teeth in the back of the mouth, with new ones replacing those worn down from the continual chewing of vegetation. *Anatosaurus* reached a height of about eighteen feet. The heavy flat tail served both as a balancing device and as a propulsive organ for swimming. Excellent mummified specimens of this dinosaur have provided much information about the creature's external appearance. (*See* CLAOSAURUS, THESPESIUS, TRACHODON.)

ANCHICERATOPS—*Cer., Cerat., U. Cret.* A short-crested North American giant, this genus is similar to *Eoceratops;* however, in the former, the fontanelles of the shield are not as large. Superficially, *Anchiceratops* is not too unlike its ancestor *Chasmosaurus.* It has three horns—two relatively large ones above the eyes and a small one over the nose. The dinosaur was discovered in the Edmonton Formation of Alberta, Canada.

ANCHISAURIPUS—*U. Trias.* The term was given to particular footprints found in the Connecticut Valley. The tracks are three-toed, with an additional small digit toward the rear. Apparently the animal that made the tracks was large and massive, either *Anchisaurus* or an extremely similar genus.

Skull of *Anatosaurus edmontoni.* (After Ostrom.)

ANCHISAURUS—*Ther., Theco., U. Trias.* (*Amphisaurus; possibly Megadactylus or Yaleosaurus.*) From the Connecticut Valley, *Anchisaurus* was a primitive prosauropod that probably subsisted both on meat and plants. The blunt teeth indicate that its diet was more herbivorous than carnivorous. Although it somewhat resembled the coelurosaurs, this dinosaur's short feet and heavy, stout limbs clearly indicate its membership among the later prosauropods, like the giant *Plateosaurus.* (*See* MEGADACTYLUS, YALEOSAURUS.)

ANKISTRODON—(*See* EPICAMPODON.)

ANKYLOSAURUS—*Ank., Nod., U. Cret.* (*Stereocephalus; possibly Euoplocephalus.*) This North American dinosaur exemplified the suborder Ankylosauria. The body was completely protected by a shell-like mass of bony plates. The tail, ending in a heavy club, could be swung at enemies with fatal effect. *Ankylosaurus* was virtually invulnerable unless turned upside-down. The jaws were massive, but the teeth were practically useless.

ANODONTOSAURUS—*Ank., Nod., U. Cret.* This armored dinosaur is known from imperfect specimens, including a greatly depressed skull almost one and one-fourth feet long and over a foot wide, and from a number of bones and thin armor plates. Unlike most ankylosaurs, *Anodontosaurus* had a weak lower jaw and no teeth. That, and the relative weakness of the plates, imply that the dinosaur's habits might have differed from those of most ankylosaurs. The genus was discovered in the Edmonton beds of Alberta, Canada.

ANOMOEPUS—*U. Trias.* The term was given to Connecticut Valley tracks of both hind and fore feet, indicating at least a partially quadrupedal animal. The hand, not equipped with the usual carnivore claws, has five digits. Three functional toes are on each slender hind foot.

Skull of *Anatosaurus copei.* (After Lull-Wright.)

Skeleton of the ornithopod *Anatosaurus annectens.* Courtesy of the Smithsonian Institution.

Restoration of *Anatosaurus,* the classic duck-billed dinosaur. From a painting by Zdenek Burian.

Latter portion of skull of *Anchiceratops ornatus* showing the orbital horns and shield. Courtesy of the Field Museum of Natural History.

Skull of *Anchiceratops longirostris*. Courtesy of the Geological Survey of Canada.

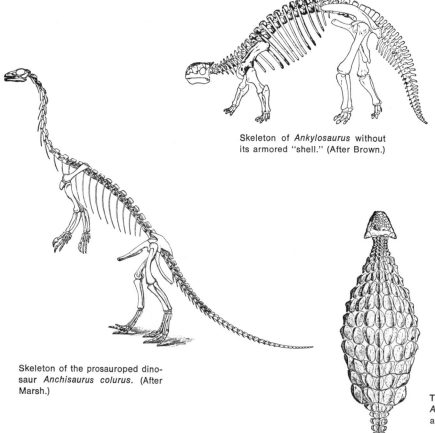

Skeleton of *Ankylosaurus* without its armored "shell." (After Brown.)

Skeleton of the prosauroped dinosaur *Anchisaurus colurus*. (After Marsh.)

Top view of skeleton of *Ankylosaurus* showing armor. (After Brown.)

Skull of the armored dinosaur *Anodontosaurus lambei.* (After Kuhn-Steel.)

Footprints of the Triassic dinosaur *Anomoepus scambus.* (After Lull.)

Richard S. Lull's conception of *Anomoepus.* (Modified after Lull.)

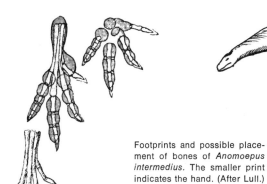

Footprints and possible placement of bones of *Anomoepus intermedius.* The smaller print indicates the hand. (After Lull.)

Restoration of the armored dinosaur *Ankylosaurus.* Courtesy of the Sinclair Oil Corporation.

Femur of the sauropod *Antarctosaurus*. Courtesy of the Field Museum of Natural History.

Skull of *Antarctosaurus wichmannianus*. (After von Huene.)

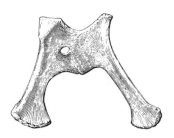

Bone of *Apatosaurus loisae*. (After Holland.)

ANOPLOSAURUS—*Orn., Iguan., L. Cret.* (*possibly Eucercosaurus, Syngonosaurus.*) This genus is known only through fossil fragments, including part of the lower jaw, humerus, femur, tibia, and other incomplete material. The fragments are from the Cambridge Greensand of England. (*See* EUCERCOSAURUS, SYNGONOSAURUS.)

ANTARCTOSAURUS—*Saur., Titan., U. Cret.* From South America and Asia, the skull of this dinosaur measures over two feet in length.

ANTRODEMUS—(*See* ALLOSAURUS.)

APATOSAURUS—*Saur., Brach., M. and U. Jur.* (*Brontosaurus; possibly Atlantosaurus.*) This giant dinosaur of both North America and Europe is undoubtedly the universal conception of a "dinosaur." *Apatosaurus* averaged seventy feet in length, with a tremendous mass of thirty tons. These titans—and similar genera—probable spent considerable time in the water, which helped to bouyantly support their weight and offer protection from the land-roaming theropods. Owing to its vulnerable construction, an *Apatosaurus* skull has never been discovered with the skeleton. However, because of skeletal similarities with *Camarasaurus*, skull casts have been fashioned patterned after the latter. (*See* ATLANTOSAURUS.)

ARCTOSAURUS—*Ther., Theco., U. Trias.* The genus is known from a cervical vertebra, resembling that in *Calamospondylus,* except for its neural spine and free cervical ribs. The specimen is from Bathurst Island in the Arctic.

ARGYROSAURUS—*Saur., Titan., U. Cret.* (*Possibly Campylodon.*) From South America, this genus is quite similar to *Titanosaurus.*

ARISTOSAURUS—*Ther., Theco., U. Trias.* (*Possibly Gryposaurus.*) Similar to *Thecodontosaurus*, this dinosaur was discovered in the Stormberg Beds of South Africa. (*See* GRYPOSAURUS.)

Leg bones of the giant sauropod *Argyrosaurus superbus*. In the center background is the femur of *Antarctosaurus*. Courtesy of the Field Museum of Natural History.

Skeleton of *Brontosaurus (Apatosaurus) excelsus*. Courtesy of the Field Museum of Natural History.

Apatosaurus lumbers toward the water which will help support its enormous mass. On the shore are Jurassic crocodilians. From a mural by Charles R. Knight. Courtesy of the Field Museum of Natural History.

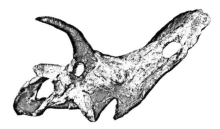

Skull of the horned dinosaur *Arrhinoceratops brachyops.* Courtesy of the Royal Ontario Museum.

Tooth of *Astrodon johnstoni.* (After Leidy.)

Tooth of *Pleurocoelus (Astrodon) valdensis.* (After Swinton.)

ARISTOSUCHUS—*Ther., Coel., L. Cret.* Known only from incomplete skeletons from the Isle of Wight, this dinosaur is quite similar to *Ornitholestes.*

ARRHINOCERATOPS—*Cer., Cerat., U. Cret.* From the Edmonton Formation of Alberta, Canada, this giant dinosaur resembles *Anchiceratops* with respect to the proportions of the large shield and nose horn. However, the shield with its two small fontanelles may have been armed with spikes. The snout is short and high. The horns above the eyes are larger than those in *Anchiceratops,* and curved forward. The skull itself is short and deep. The dinosaur rather resembles its ancestor *Chasmosaurus.*

ASIATOSAURUS—*Saur., Titan., L. Cret.* This dinosaur from Mongolia was quite similar to *Titanosaurus.*

ASTRODON—*Saur., Brach., M. and U. Jur.* Known from specimens found in North America, Portugal and England, the animal reached a length of about ten and one-half feet.

ATLANTOSAURUS—*Saur., Brach. or Titan., U. Jur.* (*Possibly Apatosaurus.*) From Colorado and Wyoming, this genus is known only from some fragments and a six-foot long femur, indicating a total length of seventy or eighty feet. (*See* APATOSAURUS.)

AUBLYSODON—*Ther., Tyrann. U. Cret.* This giant North American carnosaur is either very closely related to or synonymous with *Gorgosaurus.* (*See* GORGOSAURUS.)

AUSTROSAURUS—*Saur., Brach., L. Cret.* This dinosaur, known only from fragments, was discovered in Australia.

AVALONIA—*Ther., U. Trias.* This is a very old term given to a fossil tooth discovered in South Wales. The fossil has also been named *Zanclodon cambrensis.* (*See* ZANCLODON.)

AVIPES—*Ther., Coel., U. Trias.* This coelurosaur was discovered in Europe.

Skeleton of the sauropod dinosaur *Astrodon nanus.* (After Lull.)

Left femur of the giant dinosaur *Atlantosaurus im-manis*. (After Marsh.)

A scene of the Upper Cretaceous. The carnivorous *Aublysodon* stalks toward the water as the bone-head dinosaur *Stegoceras* flees. The armored *Edmontonia* waits on land along with the crested ornithopod *Corythosaurus*. The flying reptile *Pteranodon* glides over the lake. Courtesy of the Los Angeles County Museum of Natural History.

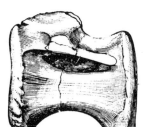

Caudal vertebra of the sauropod dinosaur
Barosaurus lentus. (After Marsh.)

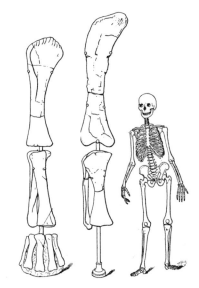

Leg and foot bones of *Bothriospondylus
madagascariensis* as compared with the
skeleton of modern man.

B

**BACTROSAURUS—*Orn., Had., U. Cret.* From Asia, this dinosaur measured over thirteen feet long and six and one-half feet high at the hips. The skull is that of a flat-headed hadrosaur, while the skeleton indicates a crested genus, leaving the matter open to speculation.

**BAHARIASAURUS—*Ther., Meg., U. Cret.* This carnosaur was discovered in North Africa.

**BAROSAURUS—*Saur., Titan., M. and U. Jur.* The powerful neck vertebrae of this genus measures over a yard long, while those of the tail are relatively short. The caudal vertebrae resemble but are proportionally not as long as those in *Diplodocus,* with chevrons lacking the anterior projections of the latter. *Barosaurus* has been found in South Dakota and East Africa.

**BASUTODON—(*See* EUSKELOSAURUS.)

**BATHYGNATHUS—The term was originally given in 1854 to a partial lower jaw containing seven teeth and described as the earliest evidence of Canadian dinosaur life. The fossil has since been identified as that of a Lower Permian pelycosaur.

**BETASUCHUS—*Ther., possibly Ornith., U. Cret.* This coelurosaur was discovered in Europe.

**BOTHRIOSPONDYLUS—*Saur., Brach., M. and U. Jur.* Found in Europe and Madagascar, this genus is similar to *Cetiosaurus* with respect to the skull and vertebrae. The teeth are large, from two to three inches long. The forelimbs are as long as the hind legs. In life the animal attained lengths of from forty-nine to over sixty-five and one-half feet.

**BRACHIOSAURUS—*Saur., Brach., M. and U. Jur.* The most massive, yet not longest, animal ever to walk the earth, *Brachiosaurus* weighed approximately fifty tons and attained lengths of seventy or eighty feet, with a height of forty feet. It is shaped rather curiously.

The front legs are longer than those behind, so that the body slopes down in the back, terminating in a proportionately short tail. The nostrils are placed atop a raised mound above the eyes, allowing most of the creature's head to submerge below the surface of the water while normal respiration was maintained. *Brachiosaurus* was found in North America, Europe, and Africa.

BRACHYCERATOPS—*Cer., Cerat., U. Cret.* From Montana, this six-foot-long dinosaur resembles *Protoceratops,* with the added adornment of a modest horn above the snout. It has been argued by some paleontologists that *Brachyceratops* is really not a separate genus at all, but a young form of *Monoclonius,* another dinosaur from the same beds. (*See* MONOCLONIUS.)

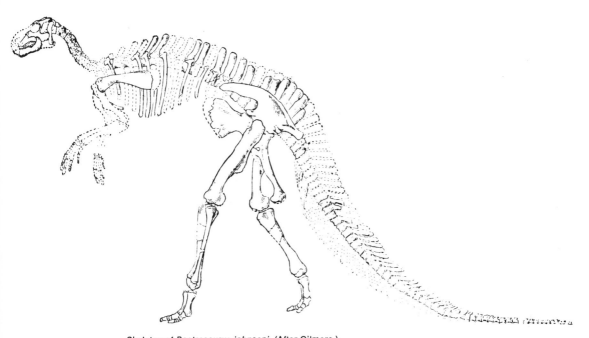

Skeleton of *Bactrosaurus johnsoni.* (After Gilmore.)

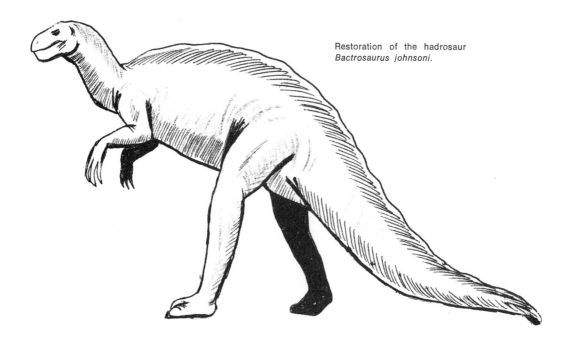

Restoration of the hadrosaur
Bactrosaurus johnsoni.

Skeleton of the horned dinosaur *Brachyceratops montanensis.* Courtesy of
the Smithsonian Institution.

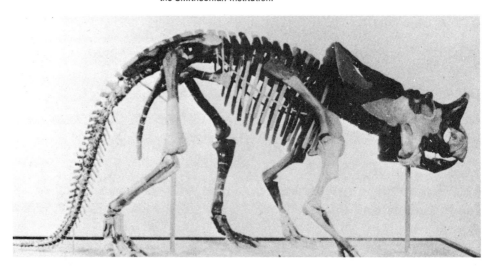

BRACHYLOPHOSAURUS—*Orn., Had., U. Cret.* This North American hadrosaur has a rather rounded bill and an extremely small crest.

BRACHYPODOSAURUS—*Ank., Nod., U. Cret.* Discovered in the Lameta beds of Jubbulpore, Madhya-Pradesh, India, this armored dinosaur is very imperfectly known from a short left humerus.

BRASILEOSAURUS—*Ther., Coel., L. Cret.* Known only from fragments found in South America, this genus is apparently closely related to *Elaphrosaurus*.

BRONTOSAURUS—(*See Apatosaurus.*)

BRONTOZOUM—*Trias.* The name *Brontozoum* has been given to three-toed tracks, including the imprint of a tail, discovered in sandstone in England.

Skull of the hadrosaur *Brachylophosaurus canadensis*. (After Ostrom.)

Model of *Brachyceratops* by C. W. Gilmore. Courtesy of the Smithsonian Institution.

Skeleton of the enormous sauropod *Brachiosaurus brancai* in the Berlin Museum.

Restoration of *Brachiosaurus* supported buoyantly by the water.
From a painting by Zdenek Burian.

Femur of *Brachiosaurus altithora*. Courtesy of
the Field Museum of Natural History.

Footprints of *Brontozoum*.
(After Marsh.)

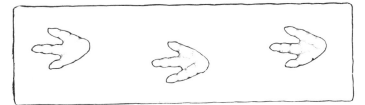

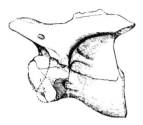

Cervical vertebra of the coelurosaur *Calamospondylus foxi.*

C

CAENAGNATHUS—*Ther., Ornith. or possibly a separate family named Caenagnathidae, U. Cret.* This genus of dubious classification was discovered in North America.

CALAMOSAURUS—(*See* CALAMOSPONDYLUS.)

CALAMOSPONDYLUS—*Ther., Coel., L. Cret. (Calamosaurus.)* This coelurosaur was discovered in Europe.

CAMARASAURUS—*Saur., Brach., M. and U. Jur. and L. Cret.* (**Probably** *Morosaurus;* **possibly** *Uintasaurus.*) This small sauropod from North America and Europe was only eighteen to thirty feet long—small when compared to giants like *Apatosaurus* and *Diplodocus.* The skull is lightly built and was quite ventillated. It has been theorized that *Camarasaurus* might actually be a young form of a larger adult, such as *Apatosaurus.* The animal flourished generally during the Jurassic, but in Europe managed to survive through the Lower Cretaceous. (*See* APATOSAURUS, MOROSAURUS, UINTASAURUS.)

CAMPOTONODUS—(*See* CAMPTOSAURUS.)

CAMPTONOTUS—(*See* CAMPTOSAURUS.)

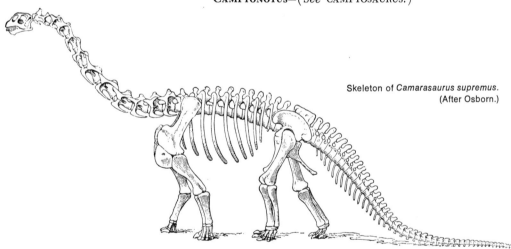

Skeleton of *Camarasaurus supremus.*
(After Osborn.)

Skeleton of *Camarasaurus lentus*. Courtesy of Dinosaur National Monument
and the Smithsonian Institution.

Model of the sauropod dinosaur *Camarasaurus* by C. W. Giimore. Courtesy
of the Smithsonian Institution.

Tooth of *Camptosaurus medius.*
(After Kuhn-Steel.)

CAMPTOSAURUS—*Orn., Iguan., M. and L. Jur.* (*Camptonodus, Camptonotus, Cumnoria.*) A very early ornithischian dinosaur, *Camptosaurus*, a descendent of a thecodont line, was to be the ancestor of all future dinosaurs of this order. The animal was small, with species ranging from four to fifteen feet in length. The heavy hind legs indicate that the reptile was essentially bipedal. However, the broad fingers imply that at least some quadrupedal locomotion occurred. *Camptosaurus* flourished both in North America and in Europe. The greatest abundance of skeletons has been encountered in Wyoming.

CAMPYLODON—(*See* ARGYROSAURUS.)

CARCHARODONSAURUS—*Ther., Meg., U. Cret.* From the Sahara Desert and Egypt, this carnosaur attained a length of approximately twenty-six and one-third feet. The teeth are sharp, curved, and equipped with two ridges. The animal is typical of the large theropods, with the exception of the high back vertebrae, which are large, but nowhere near the proportions of those in *Spinosaurus.*

CARDIODON—(*See* CETIOSAURUS.)

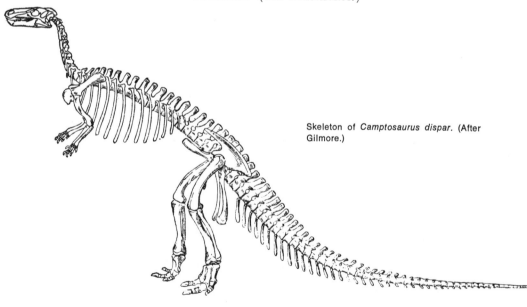

Skeleton of *Camptosaurus dispar.* (After Gilmore.)

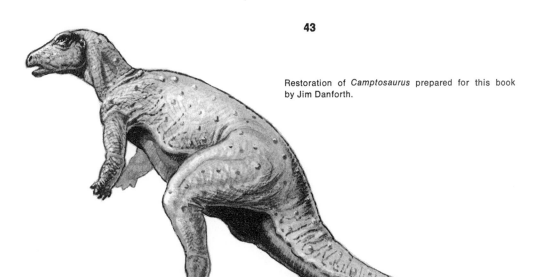

Restoration of *Camptosaurus* prepared for this book by Jim Danforth.

Skeletons of two species of *Camptosaurus*. In the foreground is *Camptosaurus browni*, in the background the smaller species *C. nanus*. Courtesy of the Smithsonian Institution.

Restoration of *Carcharodontosaurus*.

Restoration of the ceratopsian dinosaur *Centrosaurus flexus*. (Based on a model by Lull.)

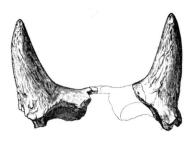

Horn cores of *Ceratops montanus*. (After Marsh.)

Restoration of the horned dinosaur *Ceratops*.

Caudocoelus—*Ther., Coel., M. and U. Jur.* This coelurosaur was discovered in Europe.

Caulodon—*Saur., Brach., M. and U. Jur.* The term was first given to fragmentary material discovered in America and now considered as synonymous with *Pelorosaurus.* (*See* Pelorosaurus.)

Centrosaurus—*Cer., Cerat., U. Cret.* Two theories concern this horned dinosaur. The first is that *Centrosaurus* is synonymous with *Monoclonius;* the second is that they are separate genera. The main criterion for the latter theory is that the long nose horn of *Centrosaurus* curves forward. Otherwise the skull is similar to that of *Monoclonius.* The dinosaur is from the Belly River formation, Alberta, Canada. (*See* Monoclonius.)

Ceratops—*Cer., Cerat., U. Cret. (Proceratops.)* Known from incomplete skeletons, this genus has been found in Montana and Colorado. The animal possessed a small shield and three horns, the nasal horn being slightly longer than those over the eyes.

Ceratosaurus—*Ther., Meg., U. Jur.* This alleged North American genus was a swift, savage, twenty-foot-long carnosaur with a peculiar distinction. Over each eye is a bony ridge, while above the nose was a horn-like growth. This deviation from the normal theropod hornless skull has led to new thinking by many paleontologists that *Ceratosaurus* is actually *Allosaurus* with an abnormal growth and that any differences in skeletal structure might be attributed to an arthritic condition. Other paleontologists claim that *Ceratosaurus* is a male form of the female *Allosaurus.* (*See* Allosaurus.)

Cetiosauriscus—(*See* Cetiosaurus.)

Cetiosaurus—*Saur., Brach., M. Jur. to L. Cret. (Cardiodon, Cetiosauriscus.)* When first described by Professor Richard Owen in 1841, *Cetiosaurus* was believed to be a giant crocodile. The genus ranged from

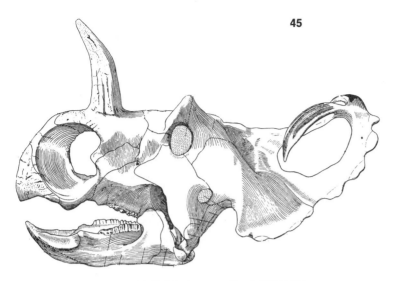

Skull of *Centrosaurus flexus.* (After Lull.)

Skeleton of the theopod dinosaur *Ceratosaurus nasicornis.* Courtesy of the Smithsonian Institution.

Model by C. W. Gilmore of *Ceratosaurus nasicornis* feeding on the herbivorous dinosaur *Camptosaurus nanus.* Courtesy of the Smithsonian Institution.

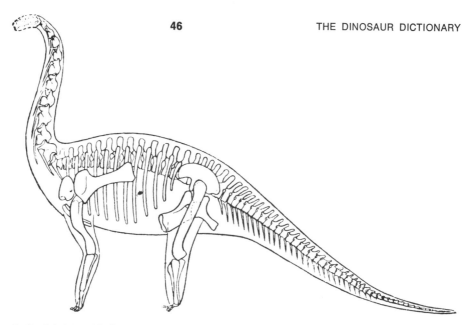

Outlined skeleton of *Cetiosaurus oxoniensis*.
(After von Huene.)

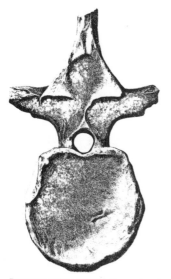

Dorsal vertebra of *Cetiosaurus brevis*.
(After Owen.)

Restoration of the giant sauropod dinosaur *Cetiosaurus* by
Neave Parker. Courtesy of the British Museum (Natural
History.)

fifty to sixty feet in length. Unlike the later sauropods, the vertebrae has a spongy texture. *Cetiosaurus* has been found in the Middle Jurassic of Africa and Middle Jurassic and Lower Cretaceous of Peterborough and Oxfordshire, in southern England.

CHASMOSARUS—*Cer., Cerat., U. Cret. (Protorosaurus.)* The long-frilled ceratopsians from the Lance and Edmonton sediments evolved from this genus, or some similar, undiscovered dinosaur. *Chasmosaurus,* a relative of *Monoclonius* and *Styracosaurus,* has a long shield with large fontanelles. A small horn is situated above the nose while two medium-sized horns are above the eyes. *Chasmosaurus* was discovered in the Belly River beds of Alberta, Canada.

CHEIROSTENOTES—(*See* CHIROSTENETES.)

CHEIROTHERIUM—*L. Trias.* The term was given to numerous tracks found in both North America and Europe. These prints might belong to early dinosaurs, but could also be those of the more primitive pseudosuchians. The controversy mainly involves the fact that no dinosaur bones have been identified from the Lower Triassic.

CHENEOSAURUS—*Orn., Had., U. Cret.* From the Edmonton beds of Canada, this crested, duck-billed dinosaur was of moderate size. The skull resembles that of *Procheneosaurus* and is rather large in comparison to the skeleton. However, the skull is relatively small when compared to other hadrosaurs from the same formation. The short crest appears as a bump over and slightly in front of the eyes.

Femur of
Cetiosaurus longus.

Tooth of *Cetiosaurus leedsi.*
(After Swinton.)

The ceratopsian dinosaur *Chasmosaurus* cautiously retreats from the fifty-foot-long crocodile *Phobosuchus.* Restoration by Walter Ferguson. Courtesy of the American Museum of Natural History.

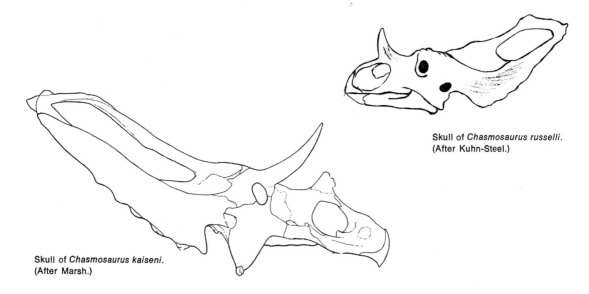

Skull of *Chasmosaurus russelli.*
(After Kuhn-Steel.)

Skull of *Chasmosaurus kaiseni.*
(After Marsh.)

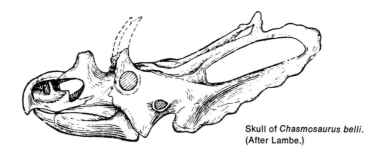

Skull of *Chasmosaurus belli.*
(After Lambe.)

Skull of *Chasmosaurus brevi-
rostris.* After Kuhn-Steel.)

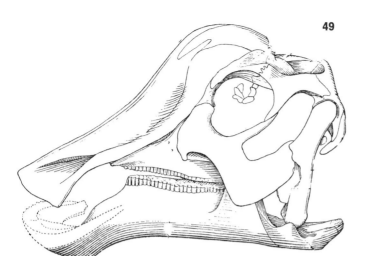

Skull of the duck-billed dinosaur
Cheneosaurus tolmanensis. (After Lull-Wright.)

CHIALINGOSAURUS—*Steg., Stego., M. or U. Jur.* This relatively slender stegosaur is known from fragmentary material, including a left femur, limb bones, vertebrae, dermal spines, and others. The primitive genus seems to be an evolutionary link between *Scelidosaurus* and *Kentrosaurus*, the spines being small and plate-like.

CHIAYÜSAURUS—*Saur., Brach. or Titan., U. Cret.* The term was given to some fossil teeth found in Kansas and eastern Asia that may actually belong to *Euhelopus.* (*See* EUHELOPUS.)

CHIENKOSAURUS—(*See* CHIENLEOSAURUS.)

CHIENLEOSAURUS—*Ther., Meg., M. and U. Jur. (Chienkosaurus.)* This carnosaur was discovered in Asia.

CHILANTHIOSAURUS—*Ther., Meg., L. and U. Cret.* This carnosaur was discovered in eastern Asia.

CHINGKANKONSAURUS—*Ther., possibly Tyrann., U. Cret.* This carnosaur was discovered in eastern Asia.

Tooth of *Cladeiodon lloydi.* (After Owen.)

Restoration of the stegosaur *Chialingosaurus* by Neave Parker. Copyright the *Illustrated London News.*

CHIROSTENOTES—*Ther., Ornith., U. Cret.* This coelurosaur was discovered in Alberta, Canada. The genus is known primarily from some finger bones, plus a light mandible.

CHONDROSTEOSAURUS—(*See* PELOROSAURUS.)

CINODON—(*See* CIONODON.)

CIONODON—*Orn., Had., U. Cret. (Cinodon.)* The term was given to fragmentary material of doubtful identity. A right maxillary bone with teeth attributed to *C. stenopsis* cannot be found in the American Museum collection where it was supposedly placed; it is not listed in the catalogue. The material is from Colorado and Alberta, Canada. The genus may be synonymous with *Thespesius.* (*See* THESPESIUS.)

CLADEIODON—*Ther., possibly U. Trias. (Abalonia, Cladyodon, Kladeisteriodon, Smilodon.)* The genus is questionably known by a tooth, discovered in England, resembling that of *Zanclodon,* only more slender.

CLADYODON—(*See* CLADEIODON.)

CLAORHYNCHUS—*Orn., Had., U. Cret.* From the Judith River formation of Montana, this genus is imperfectly known from a predentary and a partial premaxilla. Once believed to be the bones of a ceratopsian, they are now presumed to be hadrosaurian.

CLAOSAURUS—*Orn., Had., U. Cret.* Claosaurus has the distinction of being the oldest known hadrosaur of North America. In appearance, the genus resembles the typical hadrosaurs, although it is relatively smaller (about twelve feet in length) and with a considerably longer tail. The first metatarsal is present, a characteristic of the iguanodonts instead of the hadrosaurs. The skull has not been preserved, but jaw fragments indicate the primitive state of the teeth. One species originally named *C. annectens* has since been identified as a type of *Anatosaurus.* (*See* ANATOSAURUS.)

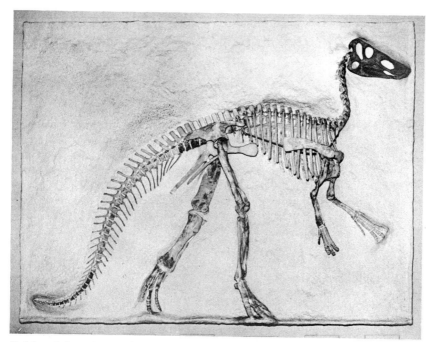

Skeleton of the ornithopod *Claosaurus agilis*. Parts of this specimen, including the missing skull, have been restored. Courtesy of the Peabody Museum of Natural History, New Haven.

CLARENCEIA—*Ther., possibly a member of a separate family, Ornithosuchidae, U. Trias.* This primitive carnosaur was discovered in South Africa.

CLASMODOSAURUS—*Saur., uncertain family classification, U. Cret.* Known primarily from fossil teeth, this genus was discovered in South America.

CLASMOSAURUS—(*See* GENYODECTES.)

CLEPSYSAURUS—*U. Trias.* The term was given in 1851 to a few bones discovered in Lehigh County, Pennsylvania, and attributed to a coelurosaur. The genus is now classified as a thecodont of the suborder Phytosauria.

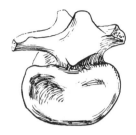

Dorsal vertebra of *Coeluroides largus.*
(After von Huene.)

Restoration of the coelurosaur *Coelophysis* by R. Freund.

COELOPHYSIS—*Ther., Hall., U. Trias.* From New Mexico, this early coelurosaur, which grew to lengths of eight to ten feet, resembles its thecodont ancestors. *Coelophysis* was light, agile and not more than fifty pounds in weight. The bones are hollow and somewhat thin, and the creature could easily run on its birdlike legs. The legs, neck and tail are all long and slender. The long jaws are filled with numerous small but sharp teeth, suitable for trapping its prey. It is possible that, unlike most dinosaurs, *Coelophysis* did not lay eggs but bore its young alive.

COELOSAURUS—*Ther., Coel., U. Cret.* This coelurosaur was discovered in North America.

COELUROIDES—*Ther., Coel., U. Cret.* This coelurosaur was discovered in southern Asia.

COELURUS—(*See* ORNITHOLESTES.)

COLUMBOSAURIPUS—*L. Cret.* The term was given to tracks found in Canada only slightly different from *Irenesauripus,* and possibly synonymous with *Gypsichnites.* Although no bone fragments were found in the vicinity for verification, the tracks appear to be of an ornithopod like *Camptosaurus.* The stride indicates that the animal was relatively swift.

COMPSOGNATHUS—*Ther., Coel., M. and U. Jur.* From central Europe, *Compsognathus* maintains the distinction of being the smallest known genus of dinosaur. This coelurosaur was no larger than a chicken. A particular skeleton from southern Germany "contains" an incomplete skeleton of an apparently even smaller dinosaur, indicating that either *Compsognathus* bore its young alive or that it was a cannibal. The main diet of this miniature dinosaur probably consisted of small reptiles and mammals.

COMPSOSUCHUS—*Ther., Coel., U. Cret.* This coelurosaur was discovered in Asia.

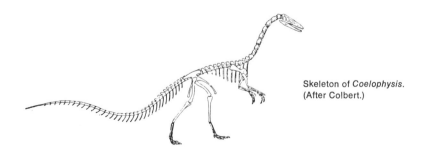

Skeleton of *Coelophysis.*
(After Colbert.)

Restoration of the tiny dinosaur *Compsognathus*. From a mural by
Charles R. Knight. Courtesy of the Field Museum of Natural History.

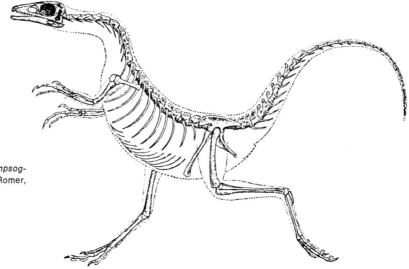

Outlined skeleton of *Compsognathus longipes*. (After Romer,
Heilmann.)

Cervical vertebra of *Composuchus solus*.
(After von Huene.)

CORYTHOSAURUS—*Orn., Had., U. Cret.* This hadrosaur from the Edmonton beds of Alberta, Canada, has an extremely large helmet-shaped crest occupying the entire area of the top of the skull. Formed by the premaxillary and nasal bones, this crest is hollow. In life, the dinosaur attained lengths of approximately twenty-six feet. It has been suggested that *Corythosaurus* might actually be the male form of *Diclonius*. (*See* THESPESIUS.)

CRASPEDODON—*Orn., Iguan., U. Cret.* From Belgium, this genus is similar to *Iguanodon*, yet with some differences, primarily in the teeth. The teeth of *Craspedodon* are five-ridged, laterally compressed and better adapted for chewing than those of *Iguanodon*.

CRATAEOMUS—(*See* STRUTHIOSAURUS.)

CRATEROSAURUS—*Steg., Stego., L. Cret.* The genus is known from a partial dorsal neural arch discovered in Bedfordshire, England. The specimen was first described as part of a skull.

CREOSAURUS—*Ther., Megal., U. Jur.* The term was given to two skulls, each over two and one-half feet long. The North American genus is very similar to or synonymous with *Allosaurus*. (*See* ALLOSAURUS.)

CRYPTODRACO—*Orn., Iguan., M. Jur. (Cryptosaurus.)* This iguanodont is known only from a femur discovered in the Oxford Clay of Great Gransden, England.

CRYPTOSAURUS—(*See* CRYPTODRACO.)

CUMNORIA—(*See* CAMPTOSAURUS.)

D

DACENTRURUS—(*See* OMOSAURUS.)

DANUBRIOSAURUS—(*See* STRUTHIOSAURUS.)

DASYGNATHOIDES—(*See* ORNITHOESUCHUS.)

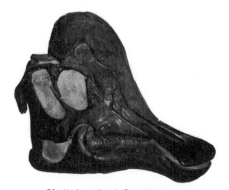

Skull (cast) of *Corythosaurus brevicristatus*. Photograph by the author. Courtesy of the Los Angeles County Museum of Natural History.

Restoration of the crested dinosaur *Corythosaurus*. Courtesy of
the Sinclair Oil Corporation.

Skull of *Corythosaurus casuarius*.
(After Lull-Wright.)

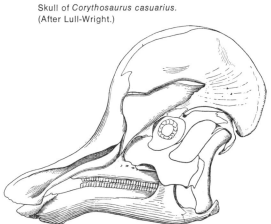

Skeleton of *Corythosaurus intermedius*. Courtesy of the Academy of Natural Sciences
of Philadelphia.

Skull of *Corythosaurus bicristatus.*
(After Lull-Wright.)

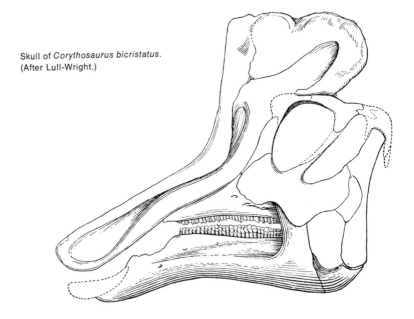

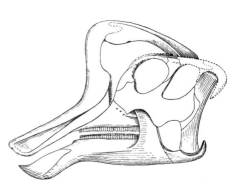

Skull of *Corythosaurus frontalis.*
(After Parks.)

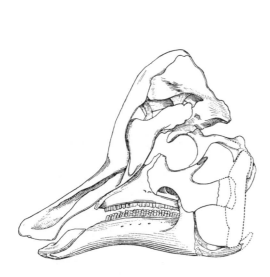

Skull of *Corythosaurus excavatus.*
(After Lull-Wright.)

DEINODON—*Ther., Tyrann., U. Cret. (Dinodon.)* The term was given to a left dentary almost twenty inches long and some fossil teeth found at the San Juan River, Utah. The tooth sockets correspond in number to those in *Tyrannosaurus*. The general form of the dentary, however, resembles that of *Albertosaurus,* although the number of teeth is different. In actuality, *Deinodon* is probably synonymous with *Gorgosaurus*. (*See* GORGO-SAURUS.)

DICERATOPS—*Cer., Cerat., U. Cret.* The term was given to a skull possibly synonymous with *Triceratops hatcheri*. The horns above the eyes are relatively short and erect, curving forward slightly. The nasal horn is not fully developed and the shield is quite broad. As no other examples of *Diceratops* have been found other than this skull, some paleontologists believe the differences from *Triceratops* to be pathological instead of genetic. (*See* TRICERATOPS.)

DICLONIUS—*Orn., Had., U. Cret.* The term has been given to a number of presumably hadrosaurian teeth, discovered in Montana's Judith River formation. One species, *D. perangulatus,* is probably the tooth of a ceratopsian, although it has also been called synonymous with *Trachodon mirabilis*. The genus is probably synonymous with *Thespesius*. (*See* THESPESIUS, TRACHODON.)

DICRAEOSAURUS—*Saur., Titan., M. and U. Jur.* From Tendaguru, Tanganyika Territory, Africa, this genus resembles *Diplodocus,* only on a smaller scale. *Dicraeosaurus* grew to approximately forty-three feet long. The neck is of only moderate length. The vertebrae lack lateral pits and are not as cavernous as those in *Camarasaurus;* and the neural spines are relatively high.

DIDANODON—*Orn., Had., U. Cret.* (*See* PROCHENEOSAURUS, THESPESIUS.)

DIMODOSAURUS—(*See* PLATEOSAURUS.)

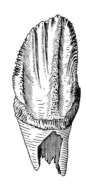

Tooth of *Craspedodon lonzeensis*. (After Dollo.)

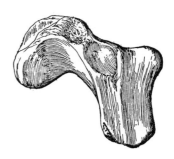

Fragmentary bone of *Craterosaurus*. (After Nopsca.)

Skull of the theropod dinosaur *Creosaurus atrox*. (After Osborn.)

Femur of *Cryptodraco eumerus*. (After Seeley.)

Skull of the carnivorous dinosaur *Deinodon loncinator*. (After Maleev.)

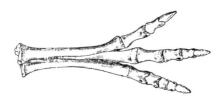

Hand bones of *Deinodon novojilovi*. (After Maleev.)

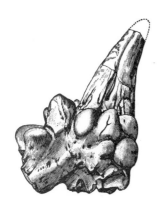

Fossil labeled as *Diclonius*. (After Marsh.)

DINODOCUS—*Saur., Brach., Jur.* Known from fragments, including a partial humerus, discovered in England, this genus might be synonymous with *Ornithopsis* and is probably identical with *Pelorosaurus*. The dinosaur was probably quite large with slender forelimbs. (*See* ORNITHOPSIS, PELOROSAURUS.)

DINODON—(*See* DEINODON.)

DINOSAURUS—(*See* GRESSLYOSAURUS.)

DIPLODOCUS—*Saur., Titan., M. and U. Jur.* Although relatively lightweight when compared with *Apatosaurus and Brachiosaurus,* this slender genus of some twenty-six tons or less has the distinction of being the longest known dinosaur, its length approaching ninety feet. This fantastic length may be greatly attributed to the tremendous, snaky neck and the long whip-like tail. The head of *Diplodocus* is almost ridiculously small. The nostrils are placed on top to allow most of the head to submerge below the water's surface and the teeth are meager pegs. The genus was discovered in the Morrison beds of western North America.

DIRACODON—*Steg., Stego., U. Jur.* From North America, this genus is considered by some paleontologists to be a young form of *Stegosaurus*. However, in *Diracodon* the intermedian and ulnar bones of the forefoot are separate. In *Stegosaurus* these are co-ossified together. (*See* STEGOSAURUS.)

DOLICHOSAURUS—*Ther., Hall., U. Trias.* This coelurosaur was discovered in Europe.

DORYPHOROSAURUS—(*See* KENTROSAURUS.)

DROMAEOSAURUS—*Ther., probably Coel., U. Cret.* The North American genus is known from an incomplete skull and some bone fragments. The teeth are well developed. The jaws are long but not massive. The skull, of which the top is fragmentary, is slightly larger than that of *Struthiomimus (Ornithomimus) altus* and is of the general proportions of that of

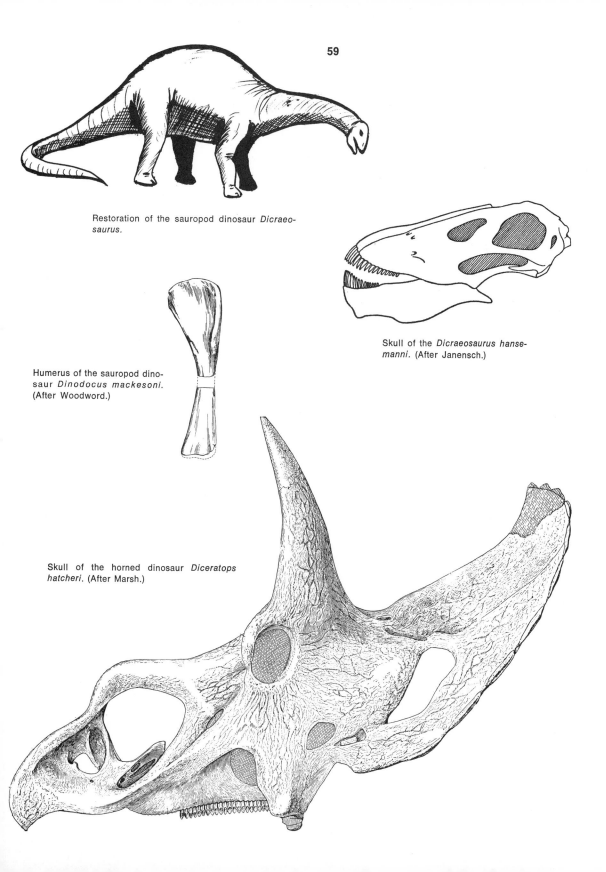

Restoration of the sauropod dinosaur *Dicraeosaurus.*

Humerus of the sauropod dinosaur *Dinodocus mackesoni.*
(After Woodword.)

Skull of the *Dicraeosaurus hanse-
manni.* (After Janensch.)

Skull of the horned dinosaur *Diceratops
hatcheri.* (After Marsh.)

Skeleton (cast) of *Diplodocus carnegii.* Courtesy of the British Museum (Natural History).

Deinodon, but with fewer teeth. Though fragmentary, the foot bones can be seen to differ from those of *Struthiomimus.*

DROMICOSAURUS—*Ther., Theco., U. Trias.* This prosauropod was discovered in the Stormberg beds of South Africa.

DRYOSAURUS—*Orn., Hyps. or Iguan., U. Jur. to L. Cret.* It had been commonly believed that *Dryosaurus* and *Laosaurus* were synonymous. The newest theory, however, classifies them as distinct from one another. Similar to, yet differing from *Camptosaurus,* this slender, graceful North American genus was ten to twelve feet long. The forelimbs are small, each hand possessing five digits. The metatarsals are long and hollow.

DRYPTOSAUROIDES—*Ther., probably Meg., U. Cret.* This carnosaur was discovered in Asia.

DRYPTOSAURUS—*Ther., Meg., U. Cret. (Laelaps.)* Known from fragments found in New Jersey, *Dryptosaurus* might be synonymous with *Allosaurus* and *Creosaurus.* It has been restored as being able to take tremendous leaps. (*See* ALLOSAURUS, CREOSAURUS.)

Skeleton of *Diplodocus longus.* Courtesy the Smithsonian Institution.

DYNAMOSAURUS—(*See* TYRANNOSAURUS.)

DYOPLOSAURUS—*Ank., Nod., U. Cret.* From North America, the skull of this genus is extremely similar to that of *Euoplocephalus,* but the squamosal bone is more pointed toward the back. The tail is very wide and massive, ending in a large club. The ilium resembles that of *Ankylosaurus.*

DYSALOTOSAURUS—*Orn., Hyps., U. Jur.* This small dinosaur from East Africa is known from partial skulls and various bones. The reptile, about the size of a large dog, resembles *Hypsilophodon.* The head had a slim snout and large eyes. The hind limbs are strong and lengthy.

DYSGANUS—*Orn., Had., U. Cret.* This genus has been established for a number of detached fossil teeth from the Judith River formation of Montana. The majority of these have since been proved not to be hadrosaurian, while the remaining specimens are questionable. The teeth of one species, *D. peiganus,* resemble those of *Hypsilophodon foxii,* but may belong to an ankylosaur. *D. haydenianus* is probably really *Ceratops* or *Monoclonius.* (*See* CERATOPS, MONOCLONIUS.)

Restoration of the incredibly long *Diplodocus.* From a painting by Zdenek Burian.

Restoration of the armored *Dyoplosaurus*. Two members of the genus *Ornithomimus* are in the background. By Neave Parker.

Skull of *Dyoplosaurus acuto-squameous*. (After Kuhn-Steel.)

Tail of *Dyoplosaurus acuto-squameous*. (After Parks.)

A lively Jurassic scene as one *Dryptosaurus* leaps to vanquish a rival. By Charles R. Knight. Courtesy of the American Museum of Natural History.

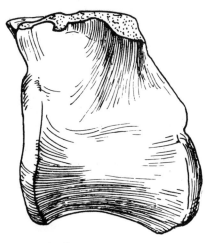

Dorsal vertebra of *Dryptosauroides grandes.* (After von Huene.)

DYSTROPHAEUS—*Saur., Brach., U. Jur.* This genus is known only from a few bones discovered in 1877 in southeastern Utah. Apparently the bones are from a rather large dinosaur.

E

ECHINODON—(*See* SAURECHINODON.)

EDMONTONIA—*Ank., Nod., U. Cret.* This North American genus is covered on the top and sides by armored plates. The nasal openings are large, while the face is covered with hard plates. The skull is long, approximately sixteen inches. The animal is extremely similar to *Palaeoscincus,* and some paleontologists believe the two genera to be synonymous. Some restorations show *Edmontonia* as a more squaty animal, corresponding to the Mongolian *Syrmosaurus.* (*See* PALAEOSCINCUS.)

EDMONTOSAURUS—*Orn., Had., U. Cret.* From the Edmonton beds of Canada, this genus has the distinction of being the largest known hadrosaur, with a length of over forty feet. Superficially, the reptile resembles

Fragmentary skeleton of the plated dinosaur *Diracodon laticeps.* (After Marsh.)

Skull of the flesh-eating dinosaur *Dromaeosaurus albertensis.* (After Brown.)

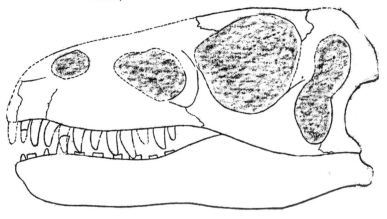

Anatosaurus. One specimen displays a crest running down the back and tail, a characteristic which may have applied to all hadrosaurs.

ELAPHROSAURUS—*Ther., Coel., M. and U. Jur.* This genus from eastern Africa is known from a partial skeleton, lacking the skull, and scattered fragments. The animal was approximately twice as large as *Ornitholestes*. The hind limbs are relatively short, with the tibia about two and one-half times as long as the femur.

ELOSAURUS—*Saur., Brach., U. Jur.* The genus may be a juvenile specimen of a larger sauropod somewhat resembling *Camarasaurus*. It is imperfectly known from fossils including a humerus, from limb bones, ribs, and a scapula. The pubis differs from that in most sauropods in its expanded backward projection. The genus was discovered in North America.

EMBASAURUS—*Ther., Meg., U. Cret.* This carnosaur was discovered in Asia.

EOCERATOPS—*Cer., Cerat., U. Cret.* Known from incomplete specimens, this genus has been found in the

Skeleton and restoration of the bird-like dinosaur *Dryosaurus altus*. Courtesy of the Carnegie Museum.

Skull of *Edmontonia longiceps*.
(After Kuhn-Steel.)

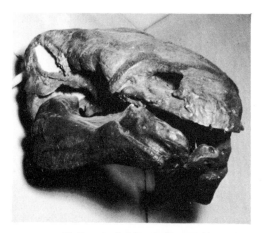

Skull cast of *Edmontonia rugosidens* after
the original in the Royal Ontario Museum.
Photograph by the author. Courtesy of the
Los Angeles County Museum of Natural
History.

Belly River formation and Red Deer River in Alberta,
Canada. The skull is short and deep, over three feet
long, and with three horns. There is one rounded,
slender horn over each eye curving slightly toward
the back at the tip, and a short horn pointing forward
above the snout.

EPANTHERIAS—*Saur., U. Jur.* This sauropod of uncertain classification was discovered in North America.

EPICAMPODON—*Possibly Ther. (Ankistrodon.)* This
genus from the Stormberg beds of South Africa has
been classified as both a coelurosaur resembling *Thecodontosaurus* and a thecodont of the suborder Pro-
terosuchia, family Chasmatosauridae.

ERECTOPUS—*Ther., Meg., L. Cret.* This carnosaur was
discovered in northern France.

EUBRONTES—*U. Trias.* The term was given to a set of
tracks found in the Connecticut Valley. The prints are
three-toed, indicating a large theropod like the European *Teratosaurus*.

EUCAMEROTUS—(*See* PELOROSAURUS.)

Model of the armored dinosaur *Edmontonia*. Courtesy of the Smithsonian Institution.

Eucerosaurus—*Orn., Iguan., L. Cret.* The term was originally given to a neutral arch and some imperfect vertebrae. This is probably synonymous with *Anoplosaurus tanyspondylus.* (*See* ANOPLOSAURUS.)

Eucnemesaurus—*Ther., Mel., U. Trias.* From Van Hoepen, South Africa, this prosauropod resembles *Zanclodon.*

Euhelopus—*Saur., Brach., L. Cret.* (*Helopus;* possibly *Chiayüsaurus.*) The genus is known primarily from a skull and a vertebral column over twelve feet long, discovered in Shantung, China. The skull, for which the precise position of the teeth is uncertain, and the pelvis resemble those of *Camarasaurus.* But the vertebrae differ. The neck of *Euhelopus* is extremely long. The animal has been restored as both quadrupedal and bipedal. (*See* CHIAYÜSAURUS.)

Euoplocephalus—*Ank., Nod., U. Cret.* The genus is known from two good skulls. The snout is large and rounded and curved in the front and along the sides. The nasal openings are large. And the front of the face is a horny beak. Some paleontologists theorize

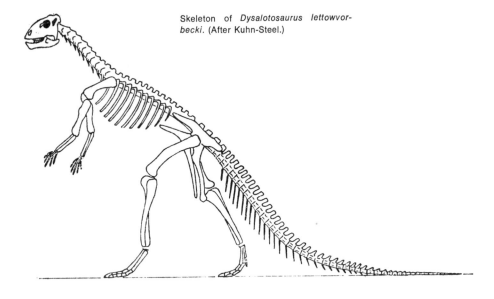

Skeleton of *Dysalotosaurus lettowvorbecki.* (After Kuhn-Steel.)

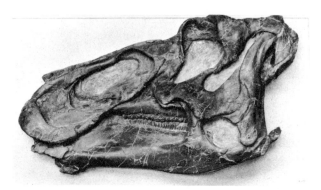

Skull of *Edmontosaurus regalis*.
Courtesy of the Field Museum of
Natural History.

Dinosaurs of the Upper Cretaceous. Several individuals of *Edmontosaurus* pause
before the armored dinosaur *Palaeoscincus*. *Corythosaurus* feeds in the water,
while in the background a herd of *Parasaurolophus* look for food. In the center
background are two individuals of the genus *Ornithomimus*. From a mural by
Charles R. Knight. Courtesy of the Field Museum of Natural History.

that this North American armored dinosaur is synonymous with *Ankylosaurus*. (*See* ANKYLOSAURUS.)

EUPODOSAURUS—*Possibly Steg., Trias.* The genus is
known only from a fragment which has also been attributed to the nothosaur *Lariosaurus*. The specimen
was discovered in Europe.

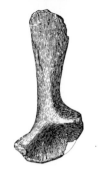

Left femur of *Elosaurus parvus*.
(After Gilmore.)

EUSKELOSAURUS—*Ther., Mel., U. Trias.* (*Orinosaurus,
Orosaurus*; possibly *Basutodon, Gigantoskelis*.) Similar in appearance to *Plateosaurus*, this prosauropod
has been found in the Stormberg beds and at Cape
Province, South Africa. (*See* GIGANTOSKELIS.)

EUSTREPTOSPONDYLUS—*Ther., Meg., M. and U. Jur.*
(*"Streptospondylus"*) This carnosaur is extremely hard
to distinguish from *Megalosaurus*. It has been found
in Middle Jurassic deposits in Madagascar, Upper
Jurassic in Europe, and throughout that period in
South America.

Vertebra of *Embasaurus minax*.

F

FABROSAURUS—*Steg., Scel., U. Trias.* This dinosaur is
known primarily from a fragmentary right mandible
containing teeth.

FULGUROTHERIUM—(*See* WALGETTOSUCHUS.)

FULICOPUS—The term was given to dinosaur footprints
found in a slab of rock from the Connecticut Valley.

G

GERANOSAURUS—*Orn., possibly Hypsil. or a separate
family, Heterodontosauridae, U. Trias.* The South
African genus is known from fragments, primarily a
partial upper jaw and mandible. Differences in the
upper jaw distinguish the genus from *Heterodontosaurus*.

GENYODECTES—*Ther., Tyrann., U. Cret.* (*Loncosaurus*;
possibly *Clasmosaurus*.) This toothless carnosaur was
discovered in Argentina.

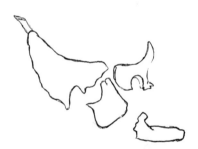

Fragmentary skull of *Eoceratops
canadensis*. (After Kuhn-Steel.)

Restoration of the horned dinosaur
Eoceratops.

Footprint of *Eubrontes giganteus*.
(After Lull.)

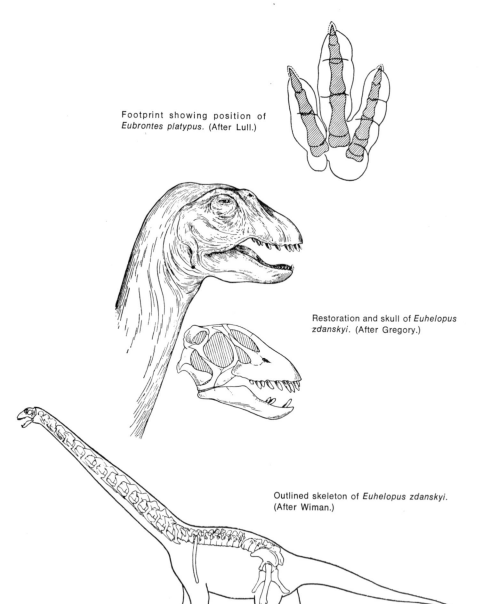

Footprint showing position of
Eubrontes platypus. (After Lull.)

Restoration and skull of *Euhelopus zdanskyi*. (After Gregory.)

Outlined skeleton of *Euhelopus zdanskyi*.
(After Wiman.)

GIGANDIPUS—*Trias.* The term has been given to tracks found in the Connecticut Valley. The animal that made them probably resembled *Teratosaurus.*

GIGANTOSAURUS—*Saur., Brach., U. Jur. (Ischyrosaurus.)* This genus is known from fragments found in the English Kimmeridge Clay. (*See* PELOROSAURUS.) Also:
—*Saur, Titan., U. Jur.* (*See* TORNIERIA.)

GIGANTOSCELIS—*Ther., Mel., U. Trias. (Gigantoscelus.)* Discovered in Van Hoepen, South Africa, this dinosaur is very similar to or possibly synonymous with *Euskelosaurus.* (*See* EUSKELOSAURUS.)

GIGANTOSCELUS—(*See* GIGANTOSCELIS.)

GORGOSAURUS—*Ther., Tyrann., U. Cret. (Teinurosaurus; probably Aublysodon, Deinodon, Dinodon.)* *Gorgosaurus* was a giant predator approximately thirty-five feet long. In superficial appearance this carnosaur appeared to be a smaller version of *Tyrannosaurus*—the almost useless hands each sporting two claws, the head enormous, and the mouth filled with sharp teeth. Though highly specialized, *Gorgosaurus* was not as specialized as *Tyrannosaurus,* whose size may have reduced it to scavenger status. *Gorgosaurus* illustrates the last stages of theropod evolution. (*See* DEINODON.)

GRESSLYOSAURUS—*Ther., U. Trias. to L. Jur. (Dinosaurus, Picrodon;* possibly *Pachysauriscus, Pachysaurops, Pachysaurus.*) This genus of uncertain classification was found in Europe. Although believed by some paleontologists to belong to the family Teratosauridae, the teeth are megalosaurian. The upper arm of this dinosaur is twice the size of the lower arm. (*See* PACHYSAURUS.)

GRYPONYX—*Ther., Theco., U. Trias.* From the Stormberg beds, Orange Free State, and Transvaal, South Africa, this prosauropod is known chiefly from bones of the hand, arms, and one very powerful claw.

GRYPOSAURUS—(*See* KRITOSAURUS.)

Skull of the armored dinosaur *Euoplocophalus titus.* (After Kuhn-Steel.)

Tooth of *Euoplocophalus magniventris.* (After Brown.)

Cervical vertebra of "*Streptospondylus*" (*Eustreptospondylus*) *major.* (After Owen.)

Fragmentary right mandible of *Fabrosaurus australis*. (After Ginsburg.)

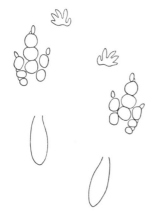

Footprints of *Fulicopus lyellianus*, made when the animal was seated. (After Lull-Wright.)

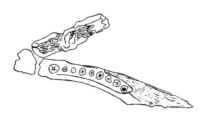

Imperfect lower jaw of *Geranosaurus atavus*. (After Brown.)

GYPOSAURUS—*Ther., Theco., U. Trias.* (Possibly *Aristosaurus, Hortalotarus*.) This prosauropod has been found in eastern Asia and in the Stormberg beds of South Africa. It reached a length of five feet.

GYPSICHNITES—*L. Cret.* The term has been given to dinosaur tracks extremely similar to or synonymous with *Columbosauripus*. (*See* COLUMBOSAURIPUS.)

H

HADROSAURUS—*Orn., Had., U. Cret.* This typical "duck-billed" dinosaur was a semiaquatic creature with a length of about forty feet. The nature of its flattened skull and jaws indicate that this ornithopod probably obtained its food in the manner of a shovel. *Hadrosaurus* has the distinction of being the first dinosaur skeleton ever unearthed in America—in New Jersey, 1858, two years after the discovery of the first dinosaur fossil fragments in Montana and South Dakota. It was described by Dr. Joseph Leidy.

HALLOPUS—*Ther., Coel. or Hall., L. Jur.* This coelurosaur, larger than *Compsognathus*, is known primarily from an incomplete skeleton discovered in Colorado. There has been some speculation that *Hallopus* also flourished during the Upper Triassic and Upper Jurassic.

HALTICOSAURUS—*Ther., Hall., U. Trias.* This European coelurosaur attained an approximate length of eighteen feet. The skull is large, the hind legs short. There are five digits on each hand, the first and fourth being small.

HAPLOCANTHOSAURUS—*Saur., Brach., M. and U. Jur.* (*Haplocanthus*.) This large dinosaur, discovered at Oil Creek, Canyon City, Colorado, is quite similar to *Cetiosaurus*. The two genera differed primarily with respect to the vertebrae. The longest skeleton of *Haplocanthosaurus* measures seventy-two feet.

HAPLOCANTHUS—(*See* HAPLOCANTHOSAURUS.)

HECATOSAURUS—(*See* ORTHOMERUS.)

HEIROSAURUS—*Ank., Nod., U. Cret. (Hierosaurus.)*
This armored dinosaur is known from one incomplete
skeleton from Kansas, of which the skull is poor. The
animal, about sixteen and one-half feet long, has the
general flattened form of *Stegopelta*. The back was
covered with plates and each side was protected by
pointed spikes, one projecting out considerably over
the others. The tail seems to have been long, slender,
and relatively flexible. As this dinosaur was discovered
in a marine formation, *Heirosaurus* may have been
somewhat aquatic.

Footprints showing possible placement of bones of *Gigandipus cau-
datus*. (After Lull.)

Richard S. Lull's conception of *Gigandipus*. (Modified after
Lull.)

The giant carnivore *Gorgosaurus libratus* mounted realistically over the hadrosaur *Lambeosaurus lambei*. Courtesy of the Field Museum of Natural History.

Model of *Gorgosaurus* standing over the defeated *Lambeosaurus* by Maidi Wiebe.
Courtesy of the Field Museum of Natural History.

Hand of the coelurosaur *Gresslyosaurus*. (After Von Huene.)

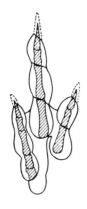

Footprint showing the possible placement of bones of *Grallator cursoria* (After Lull.)

Vertebrae of *Hadrosaurus foulkii*. (After Leidy.)

HEISHANASAURUS—*Ank., Nod., U. Cret.* This genus from Chia-yu-kuan in Northwest China is known imperfectly from material including a damaged skull, dermal plates, and fragmentary vertebrae and ribs.

HELOPUS—(*See* EUHELOPUS.)

HERRERASAURUS—*Ther., possibly Plat., Trias. (Possibly Ischisaurus.)* This primitive prosauropod was discovered in South America.

HETERODONTOSAURUS—*Orn., possibly Hypsil. or a separate family Heterodontosauridae, U. Trias.* The South African dinosaur is mainly known from a damaged skull, over three and one-half inches long with a short face, and a lower jaw. The cheek teeth have elongated crowns and are closely packed together, making them more specialized than those in *Hypsilophodon.*

HIEROSAURUS—(*See* HEIROSAURUS.)

HOPLITOSAURUS—*Ank., Acanth. or Nod., L. Cret.* This armored dinosaur from South Dakota was similar in appearance to *Polacanthus,* and is known through vertebrae, some limb bones, rib fragments, and portions of armor. When first discovered, these fossils were believed to be from a new species of *Stegosaurus*

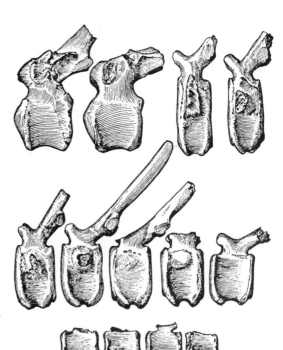

Highly inaccurate skeleton of *Hadrosaurus* (center) as it was presumed to have looked in the 1890s in this photograph of the old Field Columbian Museum. From left to right can also be seen the skeletons of extinct mammals, *Uintatherium* and the Irish Elk, and the jaws of a fossil shark. Courtesy of the Field Museum of Natural History.

Restoration of the duck-billed dinosaur *Hadro-saurus*. The individual in the water scoops up vege-tation in its shovel-like mouth. From a painting by Charles R. Knight. Courtesy of the American Mu-seum of Natural History.

or possibly a scelidosaur. Examination of the armor plates—flattened, rounded, triangular, keeled, and spined—reveals the same type of plate protection familiar to *Acantopholis, Ankylosaurus, Heirosaurus, Hylaeosaurus, Nodosaurus,* and *Stegopelta.*

HOPLOSAURUS—(*See* PELOROSAURUS.)

HORTALOTARUS—*Ther., Theco., U. Trias.* (**Possibly** ***Gyposaurus.***) This prosauropod was discovered in the Stormberg beds of South Africa.

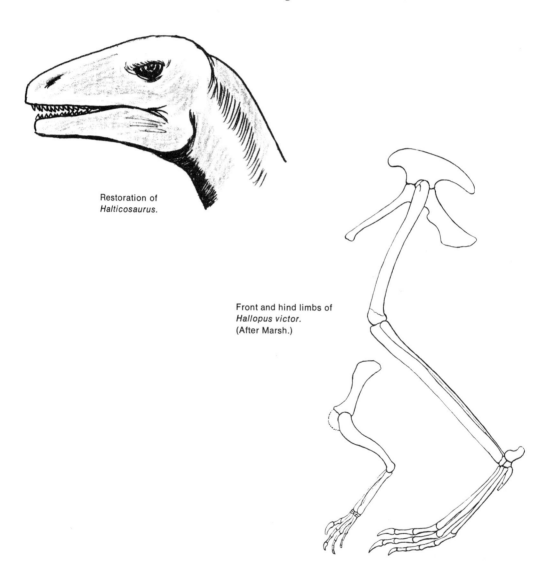

Restoration of
Halticosaurus.

Front and hind limbs of
Hallopus victor.
(After Marsh.)

Skeleton of *Haplocanthosaurus*, the only representative of this genus in the world that has been mounted for exhibit. No species has yet been given to this individual. In the background is a life-size model of the theropod *Ceratosaurus*. Courtesy of the Cleveland Museum.

Limb bone of *Haplocanthosaurus utterbacki*. (After Hatcher.)

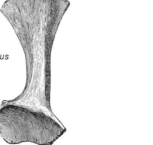

Femur of the sauropod dinosaur *Haplocanthosaurus priscus*. (After Hatcher.)

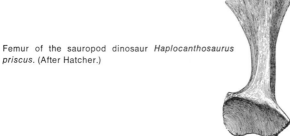

Restoration of the nodosaur *Heishanosaurus* by Neave Parker. Courtesy of the *Illustrated London News*.

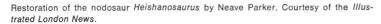

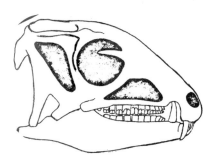

Skull of *Heterodontosaurus tucki*.
(After Kuhn-Steel.)

Tooth of *Hoplosaurus armatus*.
(After Wright.)

HYLAEOSAURUS—*Ank., Acanth., L. Cret. (Hylosaurus; possibly Regnosaurus.)* This European dinosaur is known from fragments of bones and small but strong armor plating. It has the distinction of being the third dinosaur to be discovered—in 1832. The animal may have had a series of large, hard symmetrical spines running the length of the back. (*See* REGNOSAURUS.)

HYLOSAURUS—(*See* HYLAEOSAURUS.)

HYPACROSAURUS—*Orn., Had., U. Cret.* From the Edmonton sediments of Alberta, Canada, this dinosaur had an air storage crest in the shape of a helmet, formed by the premaxillary and nasal bones, somewhat in the fashion of *Corythosaurus*. However, in the former this crest was expanded and less rounded. *Hypacrosaurus* was very large, with a skull approximately twenty-two inches high.

HYPHEPUS—*Trias.* The term has been given to tracks found in the Connecticut Valley, indicating a bipedal dinosaur probably similar to the thecodont *Saltoposuchus.*

HYPSELOSAURUS—*Saur., Titan., U. Cret. (Magyarosaurus.)* This large sauropod resembling *Apatosaurus* has been found in Transylvania and near the Rhone River in France. Among the bones from France in 1869 were numerous fossilized eggshells which were identified as either belonging to a large prehistoric bird or *Hypselosaurus*. A complete egg was discovered in 1930, eight years after the Mongolian *Protoceratops* were found and identified as dinosaur. Now with even more of such eggs unearthed in France, it has been almost certainly affirmed that they belong to *Hypselosaurus*. The genus reached an approximate length of forty feet.

HYPSIBEMA—*Orn., Had., U. Cret.* The dinosaur is known from incomplete material found in North Carolina, with vertebrae similar to those in *Hadrosaurus tripos*. The specimens are significant in showing that hadrosaurs lived in that area.

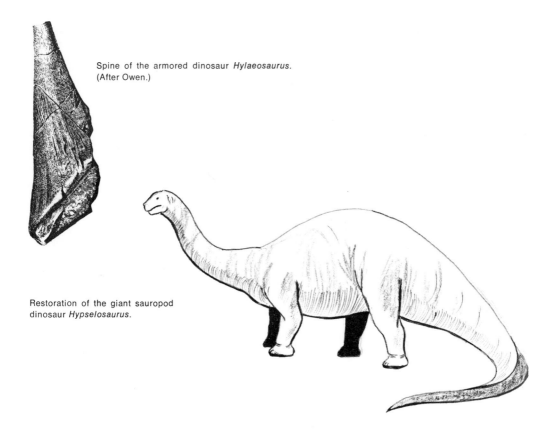

Spine of the armored dinosaur *Hylaeosaurus*.
(After Owen.)

Restoration of the giant sauropod
dinosaur *Hypselosaurus*.

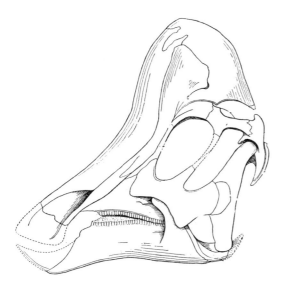

Skull of the duck-billed dinosaur *Hypa-crosaurus altispinus*. (Modified after Gilmore.)

HYPSILOPHODON—*Orn., Hyps., L. Cret.* Of all known ornithischians, this genus from the Isle of Wight is the most ancient except for *Heterodontosaurus* and various fragments. The presence of teeth in the front of the mouth and the four toes on each hind foot indicates this primitive condition. The animal was small, reaching a length of five feet. Its posture was such that the head was carried no more than two feet above the ground. It has been theorized that the long toes and fingers were used in climbing trees. The two rows of small armor scutes along the back remind one of the thecodonts and also present a connection with ancestral armored dinosaurs.

HYPSIRHOPHUS—(*See* STEGOSAURUS.)

Richard S. Lull's conception of *Hyphepus*. (Modified after Lull.)

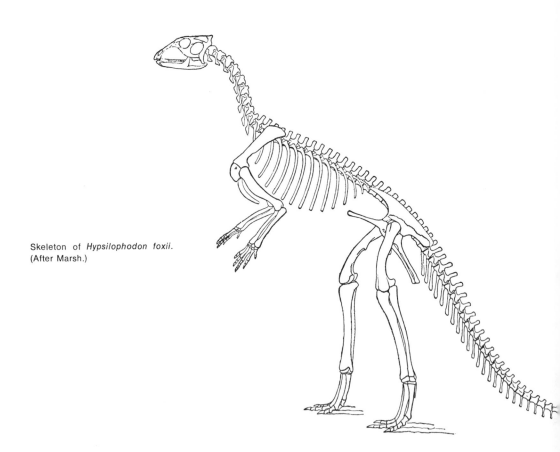

Skeleton of *Hypsilophodon foxii*. (After Marsh.)

Restoration of the ornithopod dinosaur *Hypsilophodon*, which could have spent some time in the trees. By Neave Parker. Courtesy of the British Museum (Natural History).

Maxilla of *Iguanodon orientalis.* (After Rozhdestvensky.)

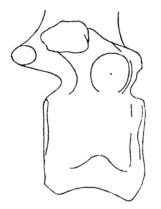

Dorsal vertebra or Iguanodon gracilis. (After Seeley.)

Mid-dorsal vertebra of *Iguanodon dawsoni.* (After Owen.)

I

**IGUANODON—*Orn., Iguan., L. Cret. (Iguanosaurus, Sphenospondylus, Therosaurus.)* From Europe, this dinosaur was originally named for some fossil teeth resembling those of the modern day lizard, the iguana. Consequently, early restorations depicted the dinosaur as a type of giant, horned, and quadrupedal iguana. It was later learned, after numerous skeletons were discovered, that *Iguanodon* was a biped. This dinosaur was strong and bulky, probably weighing seven tons, with a length of about thirty feet and a height of sixteen feet. The large spike-like thumbs have always been a curiosity. At first it was believed that these thumbs were used in combat. A more contemporary theory, however, is that the thumbs were actually used by males to attract females before mating.

IGUANOSAURUS—(*See* IGUANODON.)

ILIOSUCHUS—(*See* MEGALOSAURUS.)

INDOSAURUS—(*See* ORTHOGONIOSAURUS.)

INDOSUCHUS—(*See* ORTHOGONIOSAURUS.)

**INOSAURUS—*Ther., Meg., Cret.* This carnosaur was discovered in North Africa.

**IRENESAURIPUS—*L. Cret.* The term has been given to three-toed footprints found in the Peace River area of Canada. The tracks average fourteen and one-half inches in length. The stride averages over a yard.

ISCHISAURUS—(*See* HERRERASAURUS.)

ISCHYROSAURUS—(*See* GIGANTOSAURUS, PELOROSAURUS.)

J

**JAXARTOSAURUS—*Orn., Had., U. Cret. (Yaxartosaurus.)* From Russia, this flat-headed, solid-crested hadrosaur is known from various limb bones and vertebrae, and a partial skull.

Tooth of *Iguanodon mantelli.* (After Mantell.)

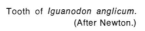

Tooth of *Iguanodon anglicum.*
(After Newton.)

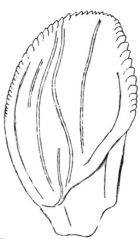

Skeleton of *Iguanodon bernissartensis.*
(After Dollo.)

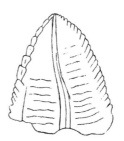

Tooth of *Iguanodon hilli.* (After
Newton.)

Skull of *Iguanodon atherfieldensis.*
(After Kuhn-Steel.)

Mandible of *Iguanodon boggii.*
(After Owen.)

Restoration of the ornithopod dino-
saur *Iguanodon* by Neave Parker.
Courtesy of the British Museum
(Natural History).

JUBBULPURIA—*Ther., Coel., U. Cret.* This coelurosaur is known only from fragments found in Asia. The genus is closely related to *Elaphrosaurus.*

K

KANGNASAURUS—*Orn., Iguan., Cret.* This iguanodont is known from a right femur, a right maxillary tooth, and possibly other incomplete material found in Bushmanland, South Africa.

KENTROSAURUS—*Steg., Stego., U. Jur. (Doryphorosaurus, Kentrurosaurus.)* From the sediments of the Lake Tanganyika area of eastern Africa, this genus, though slightly smaller, resembled *Stegosaurus.* This sixteen and one-half-foot long dinosaur is also decorated with spines and plates. In *Kentrosaurus,* however, the plates are smaller and fewer in number. The back and tail are abundant with spines.

KENTRUROSAURUS—(*See* KENTROSAURUS.)

KLADEISTERIODON—(*See* CLADEIODON.)

KOUPHICHNIUM—The term has been given to a set of small tracks in a sheet of limestone, discovered in Bavaria.

KRITOSAURUS—*Orn., Had., U. Cret. (Gryposaurus.)* The genus was found in sediments at the Belly River in Alberta, Canada, and in the Kirtland beds of New Mexico. This flat-headed hadrosaur possessed a primitive crest-like growth, an upward expansion of the nasal bone resembling a large bump in front of the eyes. It has been suggested that this dinosaur is actually the female form of *Parasaurolophus.* (*See* PARASAUROLOPHUS.)

KUANGYUANPUS—*Saur., U. Jur.* This sauropod of uncertain classification was discovered in eastern Asia.

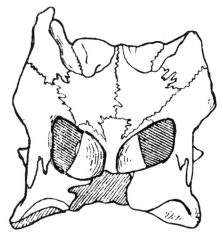

Bone of *Yaxartosaurus (Jaxartosaurus) aralensis.*

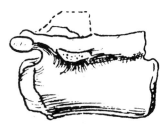

Dorsal vertebra of *Jubbulpuria tenuis.* (After von Huene.)

Right femur of *Kangnasaurus coetzei.* (After Haughton.)

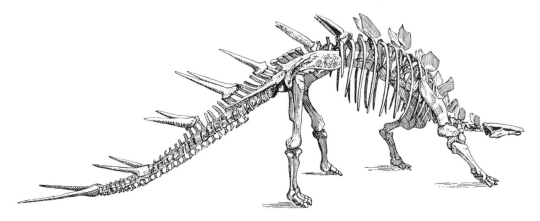

Skeleton of *Kentrosaurus aethiopicus*.
(After Janensch.)

Restoration of the stegosaur *Kentrosaurus*. Original drawing for this
book by Roy G. Krenkel.

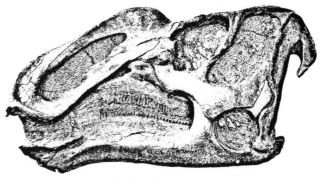

Skull of *Kritosaurus notabilis*.
Courtesy of the Geological
Survey of Canada.

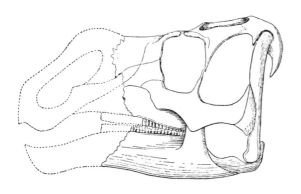

Skull of *Kritosaurus notabilis*.
(After Lambe.)

Skull of *Kritosaurus incurvimanus*.
(After Parks.)

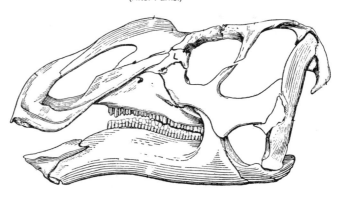

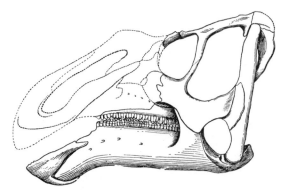

Skull of *Kritosaurus navajovius.*
(After Lull-Wright.)

Model of *Kritosaurus* by C. W. Gilmore. Courtesy of the Smithsonian
Institution.

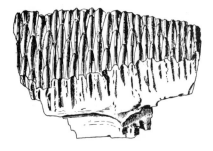

Teeth of *Trachodon (Kritosaurus)
breviceps.* (After Lull-Wright.)

L

LABROSAURUS—*Ther., Meg., U. Jur.* Known from incomplete material including jaws, teeth, pubis, and ischium, this North American genus is probably synonymous with *Allosaurus*. (*See* ALLOSAURUS.)

LAEROSAURUS—*Ther., Meg., M. and U. Jur.* Known chiefly from teeth and dentary fragments, this dinosaur is generally considered to be synonymous with *Allosaurus*. (*See* ALLOSAURUS.)

LAELAPS—(*See* DRYPTOSAURUS.)

LAEVISUCHUS—*Ther., Coel., U. Cret.* This coelurosaur is known from fragments discovered in India.

LAMBEOSAURUS—*Orn., Had., U. Cret. (Stephanosaurus.)* This hadrosaur has a hatchet-shaped crest formed by the premaxillary and nasal bones. The large genus was discovered in the Edmonton beds, Alberta, Canada.

LAMETOSAURUS—*Ank., Nod., U. Cret.* From Jubbulpore, Madhya-Pradesh, India, the genus is known from incomplete skeletal remains, including armor, a left tibia, sacrum, and ilia.

LAOSAURUS—*Orn., probably Hyps., U. Jur. and L. Cret.* (**Possibly *Dryosaurus* and one species of *Nanosaurus*.**) A North American ornithopod, this dinosaur is avian in form, with a maximum length of approximately ten feet. A complete skull of a smaller species would probably measure some three inches in length. The teeth of *Laosaurus* are small and irregular. (*See* DRYOSAURUS, NANOSAURUS.)

LAPLATOSAURUS—*Saur., Titan., U. Cret.* From South America, southern Asia, and Madagascar, this sauropod is similar to *Titanosaurus*.

LEIPSANOSAURUS—(*See* STRUTHIOSAURUS.)

LEPTOCERATOPS—*Cer., Pro., U. Cret.* Although this genus coexisted with the great horned giants, it ac-

Tooth of *Labrosaurus sulcatus.* (After Marsh.)

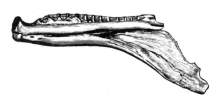

Left dentary bone of *Labrosaurus ferox.* (After Marsh.)

Pubis and ischium of *Labrosaurus fragilis.* (After Marsh.)

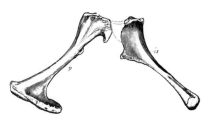

Vertebra of *Laevisuchus*.
(After von Huene.)

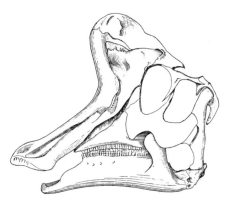

Skull of *Lambeosaurus clavinitalis*.
(After Lull-Wright.)

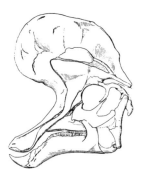

Skull of *Lambeosaurus magnicristatus*.
(After Lull-Wright.)

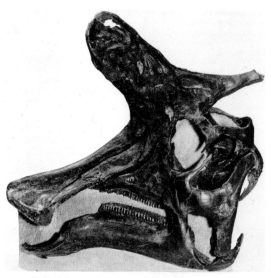

Skull of the crested dinosaur *Lambeosaurus lambei*.
Courtesy of the Field Museum of Natural History.

Model of the hadrosaur *Lambeosaurus*, killed by the carnivorous *Gorgosaurus*, which looms over it. By Maidi Wiebe. Courtesy of the Field Museum of Natural History.

Skull of *Laosaurus gracilis.*
(After Gilmore.)

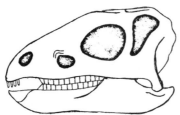

Skull of *Laosaurus altus.*
(After Kuhn-Steel.)

Sacral centrum of *Laplato-saurus madagascariensis.*
(After von Huene.)

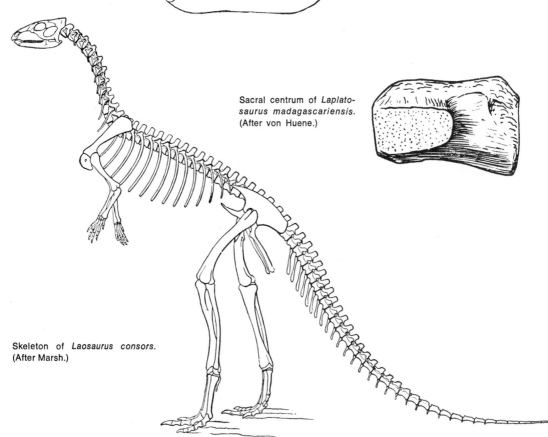

Skeleton of *Laosaurus consors.*
(After Marsh.)

tually represents an evolutionary step between *Psittacosaurus* and *Protoceratops*. It was probably able to enjoy either bipedal or quadrupedal locomotion. It shows a definite trend toward ceratopsian development, as the back of the head already sported a flat crest. The fontanelles in this shield were smaller than those in *Protoceratops*; and the feet, with all fingers present, are smaller. The beak at the end of the deep skull is similar to that of *Psittacosaurus*. *Leptoceratops* was a small dinosaur, almost four feet high, the head being almost one foot high. The genus was discovered in the Edmonton sediments, Alberta, Canada.

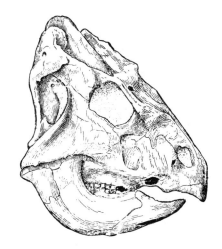

Skull of *Leptoceratops gracilis*.
(After Sternberg.)

LEPTOSPONDYLUS—(*See* MASSOSPONDYLUS.)

LEXOVISAURUS—*Steg., Stego., U. Jur.* From England and northern France, the genus had armor including plates and spines and two large spines over the hips, as found in *Kentrosaurus*. *Stegosaurus durobrivensis*, originally called *Omosaurus*, is now considered to be *Lexovisaurus*. The genus may be a direct ancestor of the later stegosaurs. (*See* OMOSAURUS, STEGOSAURUS.)

LIMNOSAURUS—(*See* ORTHOMERUS.)

LONCOSAURUS—(*See* GENYODECTES.)

LOPHORHOTHON—*Orn., Had., U. Cret.* This hadrosaur was discovered in North America.

LORICOSAURUS—*Ank., Nod., U. Cret.* The genus is imperfectly known from fragmentary bones and pieces of armor. It was discovered in South America.

LORPHORHOTHON—*Orn., Had., U. Cret.* From Dallas County, Alabama, this duck-billed dinosaur is known from an incomplete skeleton that suggests a young form of a larger adult. The skull has a crest above the nostrils, in front of the eyes. The skeleton is about forty-nine feet long.

LOUKOUSAURUS—*Ther., probably Hall., U. Trias.* This coelurosaur was discovered in eastern Asia.

LUFENGOSAURUS—*Ther., Plat., U. Trias.* Similar to *Plateosaurus*, this large prosauropod was discovered in western China.

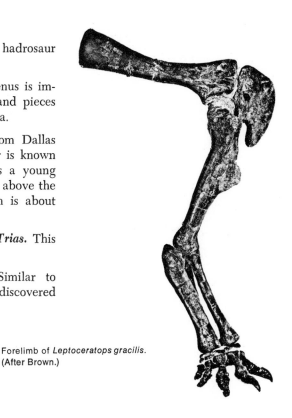

Forelimb of *Leptoceratops gracilis*.
(After Brown.)

Skull of *Lorphorhothon atopus.*
(After Kuhn-Steel.)

Foot bones of *Lufengosaurus huenei.* (After Young.)

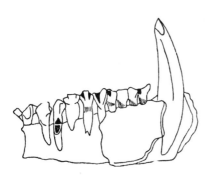

Imperfect mandible of *Lycorhinus angustidens.* (After Haughton.)

LUSITANOSAURUS—*Steg., Scelid., L. Jur.* From Portugal, this primitive stegosaur, closely related to *Scelidosaurus,* is known from a partial upper jaw.

LYCORHINUS—*Orn., Hyps. or a separate family of Heterodontosauridae, U. Trias.* From the Red Beds of South Africa, the genus is known from a partial lower jaw. Apparently this is an early ornithischian related to *Heterodontosaurus.*

M

MACHLODON—(*See* RHABDODON.)

MACRODONTOPHION—*Ther., Meg., Jur.* This carnosaur was discovered in Europe.

MACROPHALANGIA—*Ther., Ornith., U. Cret.* This coelurosaur is known from a right foot discovered in the Old Man formation, Alberta, Canada.

MACRUROSAURUS—*Saur., Titan., U. Cret.* From Cambridge, England, this sauropod is quite similar to *Titanosaurus.*

MAGNOSAURUS—*Ther., Meg., L. and U. Cret.* This dinosaur, discovered in England, is known from fragments, including vertebrae, a mandible, pubes, and tibias approximately eighteen and one-half inches long. Some paleontologists believe *Magnosaurus* to be synonymous with *Megalosaurus.* (*See* MEGALOSAURUS.)

MAGYAROSAURUS—(*See* HYPSELOSAURUS.)

MAJUNGASAURUS—*Ther., Tyrann., probably L. Cret. to U. Cret.* This carnosaur has been found in Madagascar and in the Upper Cretaceous deposits of eastern Asia.

MAMENCHISAURUS—*Saur., Titan., U. Jur.* This sauropod from eastern Asia had an exceptionally long neck. The animal in life reached an approximate length of thirty-one feet.

MANDSCHUROSAURUS—*Orn., Had., U. Cret.* (*Possibly Nipponosaurus.*) The genus is known from fragmentary material found in eastern and southeastern Asia.

The dinosaur is almost certainly a flat-headed hadrosaur. (*See* NIPPONOSAURUS.)

MANOSPONDYLUS—(*See* TYRANNOSAURUS.)

MARCELLOGNATHUS—*Orn., probably Hyps., U. Jur.* This ornithopod was discovered in North America.

MASSOSPONDYLUS—*Ther., Theco., U. Trias. (Leptospondylus, Pachyspondylus.)* This prosauropod from Asia and Africa was smaller than *Plateosaurus*. The humerus is over eight and one-half inches long, the radius about five inches, the femur almost fourteen inches, and the tibia nearly eleven and one-half inches.

Restoration of the sauropod dinosaur *Macrurosaurus*.

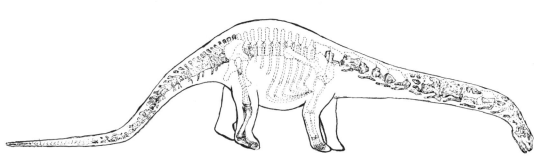

Outlined skeleton of *Mamenchisaurus constructus*. (After Young.)

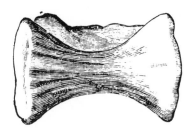

Dorsal vertebra of *Massospondylus cavinatus*.

MEGADACTYLUS—*Ther., Theco., U. Trias.* (Possibly *Amphisaurus, Anchisaurus, Yaleosaurus.*) This is an old term for a genus discovered in Springfield, Massachusetts, and usually accepted as being synonymous with *Anchisaurus.* (*See* ANCHISAURUS, YALEOSAURUS.)

MEGALOSAURUS—*Ther., Meg., L., M., and U. Jur., L. Cret.* (*Aggiosaurus, Iliosuchus;* possibly *Magnosaurus, Nuthetes, Poecilopleuron, Proceratosaurus.*) This European carnosaur of some twenty or thirty feet in length has several distinctions. It is the only

Nail of *Megalosaurus pannoniensis.* (After Lapparent.)

Restoration of the great theropod dinosaur *Megalosaurus* by Neave Parker. Courtesy of the British Museum (Natural History).

animal of its type well represented in England. It was the second dinosaur to be discovered—in 1824—in the form of some large bones, including a lower jaw with formidably sharp teeth. It was also the very first dinosaur to be described (by Dean Buckland), although it was then assumed to be a "giant" more than forty feet long. (*See* MAGNOSAURUS, NUTHETES, POECILOPLEURON, PROCERATOSAURUS.)

MELANOSAURUS—*Ther., Mel., U. Trias.* This prosauro-

Tooth of *Microceratops sulcidens.*
(After Bohlin.)

pod was discovered in the Stormberg beds of South Africa. The genus probably resembled *Zanclodon.*

METATETRAPOUS—The term was given to tracks apparently made by a dinosaur.

METRIACANTHOSAURUS—*Ther., Meg., U. Jur.* This carnosaur was, until recently, believed to be a species of *Megalosaurus (M. parkeri).* The enlongated spines and other characteristics imply a different genus altogether. *Metriacanthosaurus* was discovered in Europe.

MICROCERATOPS—*Cer., Pro., U. Cret.* From Mongolia, this genus is rather incompletely known primarily through teeth and limbs. Apparently, the genus was slender and able to move with relative swiftness.

MICROCOELUS—*Probably Saur., U. Cret.* This genus of uncertain classification was discovered in South America.

MICROSAURUS—*Saur., U. Cret.* This sauropod of uncertain classification was discovered in South America.

MONGOLOSAURUS—*Saur., Titan., L. Cret.* This sauropod was discovered in Mongolia.

MONOCLONIUS—*Cer., Cerat., U. Cret.* (**Possibly** *Brachyceratops, Centrosaurus.*) This horned giant is of the short-frilled line of ceratopsians. The shield, with two large fontanelles, is scalloped around the edges. The back of the frill often curved forward in the manner of bony hooks. Over each eye is a small horn, while above the snout stands an extremely long horn. The length of the animal in life was approximately twenty-six feet. *Monoclonius* was discovered in the Belly River sediments of Alberta, Canada. (*See* BRACHYCERATOPS, CENTROSAURUS.)

MONTANOCERATOPS—*Cer., Pro., U. Cret.* From Montana, this small ceratopsian shows a considerable degree of ceratopsian development over the similar *Protoceratops.* The feet are more developed in *Mon-*

tanoceratops. More significantly, there is a modest, yet well-developed, horn above the snout.

MORINOSAURUS—(*See* PELOROSAURUS.)

MOROSAURUS—*Saur., Brach., M. and U. Jur. and L. Cret.* This sauropod is probably the same as *Camarasaurus* (q.v.).

N

NANNOSAURUS—(*See* NANOSAURUS.)

NANOSAURUS—*Orn., Hypsil., U. Jur. (Nannosaurus)* From the Morrison formation of Colorado, the genus is known from incomplete material. This was a very small ornithopod.

NEOSAURUS—(*See* PARROSAURUS.)

NEOSODON—(*See* PELOROSAURUS.)

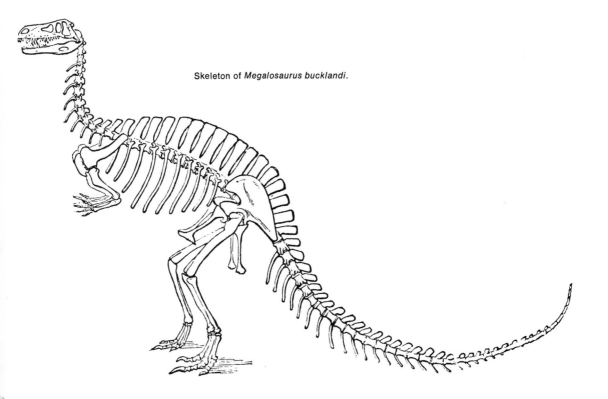

Skeleton of *Megalosaurus bucklandi.*

Restoration of the horned dinosaur *Monoclonius*. From a painting by Zdenek Burian.

NIPPONOSAURUS—*Orn., Had., U. Cret.* (Possibly *Mandschurosaurus.*) This flat-headed hadrosaur is known from an incomplete skeleton discovered on the island of Sakhalin, off the coast of Asia. The skull of this dinosaur is broad and short with a crest-like growth in the shape of a small dome. The creature was relatively small. (*See* MANDSCHUROSAURUS.)

NODOSAURUS—*Ank., Nod., U. Cret.* This North American dinosaur was completely protected by a shell-like covering of bony plates. The tail was slender and lacked the ornate deadly weapons that characterized tails of the *Ankylosaurus* and *Palaeoscincus* varieties. *Nodosaurus* attained an approximate length of seventeen and one-half feet.

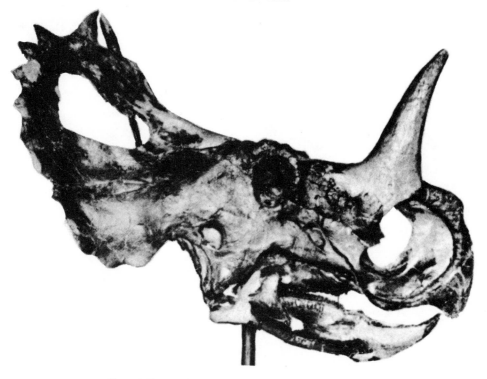

Skull of *Monoclonius nasicornis.* Courtesy of the Smithsonian Institution.

NOTOCERATOPS—*Cer., Pro. or Cerat., U. Cret.* This small ceratopsian was discovered in Patagonia, South America.

NUTHETES—*Ther., Meg., U. Jur.* Known from some small bones found in the Purbeck beds in England, this dinosaur may be synonymous with *Megalosaurus*. (*See* MEGALOSAURUS.)

O

OLIGOSAURUS—*Cer., U. Cret.* This genus of uncertain classification is known from inadequate material found in Neue Welt, Austria.

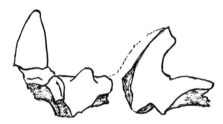

Horn cores of *Monoclonius recurvicornis.* (After Kuhn-Steel.)

Skull of *Monoclonius lowei.* (After Kuhn-Steel.)

Skull of *Monoclonius longirostris.* (After Kuhn-Steel.)

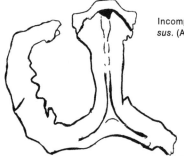

Incomplete crest of *Monoclonius crassus*. (After Kuhn-Steel.)

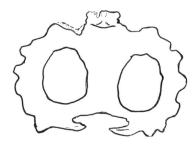

Crest of *Monoclonius apertus*. (After Kuhn-Steel.)

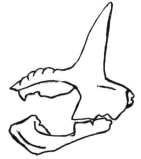

Nasal horn core and premaxilla of *Monoclonius sphenocerus*. (After Kuhn-Steel.)

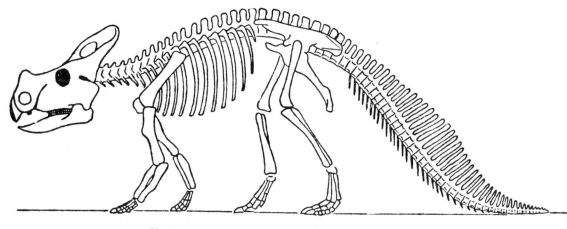

Skeleton of *Montanoceratops cerorhynchus*. (After Kuhn-Steel.)

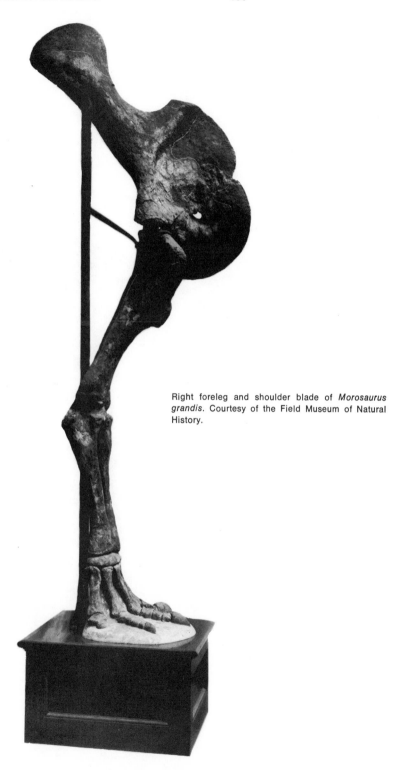

Right foreleg and shoulder blade of *Morosaurus grandis*. Courtesy of the Field Museum of Natural History.

Scapula and coracoid bones of *Morosaurus impar* in the rock where they were discovered. Courtesy of the Field Museum of Natural History.

Jaw of *Nanosaurus agilis.* (After Marsh.)

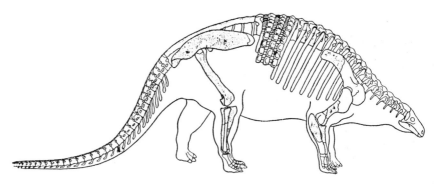

Outlined skeleton showing some armor of *Nodosaurus tectilis.* (After Lull.)

Fragmentary mandible of *Notoceratops bonavelli.* (After Huene.)

OMEISAURUS—*Saur., Brach., U. Cret.* This large sauropod was discovered in China. It is related to *Eheulopus.*

OMOSAURUS—*Steg., Stego., M. and U. Jur. (Dacentrurus, Priodontosaurus, Priodontognathus.)* From France, *Omosaurus,* or *Dacentrurus as many paleontologists prefer to call it,* is superficially quite similar to *Stegosaurus.* The main differences between the two lay in the pelvic region. The ilium of *Omosaurus* is shorter toward the back and then deepened, implying that perhaps the genera are the same, with the difference being sexual. Also, the neural arches of the dorsal vertebrae of *Omosaurus* are not as elevated as those in *Stegosaurus.* It possesses spikes, but lacks any armor plates. Eggs believed to be those of *Omosaurus* have been found in Portugal. (*See* STEGOSAURUS.)

ONYCHOSAURUS—*Ank., Acanth., U. Cret.* Discovered in Hungary, this armored dinosaur is known from inadequate material that shows armor in the region of the tail.

OPLOSAURUS—(*See* PELOROSAURUS.)

ORINOSAURUS—(*See* EUSKELOSAURUS.)

ORNITHICHNITES—*Trias.* The term has been given to bird-like three-toed tracks found in the Connecticut Valley.

ORNITHOLESTES—*Ther., Coel., U. Jur. (Coelurus.)* From the Morrison beds of North America, *Ornitholestes* was a light-weight coelurosaur built for speed. While living alongside such giants as *Allosaurus,* this small, six-foot-long theropod retained many of the superficial characteristics of its Triassic ancestors. The strong hands were equipped with three fingers, ideal for grasping its food, which consisted of small reptiles and other animals.

ORNITHOMERUS—(*See* RHABDODON.)

ORNITHOMIMUS—*Ther., Ornith., U. Cret. (Struthiomimus.)* From North America and eastern Asia, *Or-*

Pelvis of the sauropod dinosaur *Omeisaurus.* (After Young.)

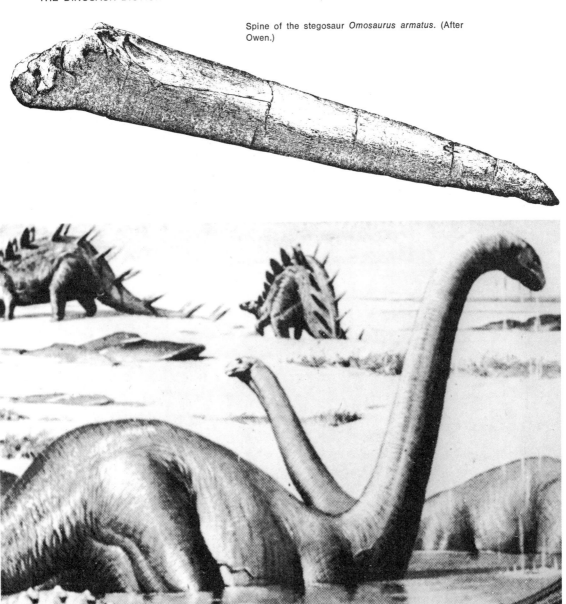

Spine of the stegosaur *Omosaurus armatus*. (After Owen.)

Restoration of the giant dinosaur *Omeisaurus*. (By Neave Parker. Courtesy of the *Illustrated London News*.)

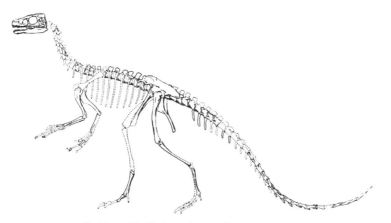

Skeleton of *Ornitholestes hermanni*.
(After Osborn.)

Restoration of the theropod dinosaur *Ornitholestes* pursuing the
first true bird *Archaeopteryx*. Courtesy of the Sinclair Oil Corporation.

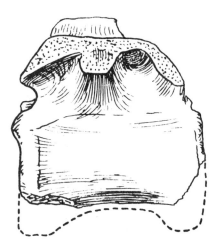

Dorsal vertebra of *Ornithomimoides (?) barasimlensis.* (After von Huene.)

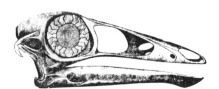

Skull of *Struthiomimus (Ornithomimus) samueli.* (After Parks.)

nithomimus was a hollow-boned coelurosaur correctly referred to as the "ostrich dinosaur." Built in such a way that it resembled the great contemporary bird, this dinosaur was fourteen feet long and seven or eight feet tall. The forelimbs are exceptionally long for a coelurosaur. And the mouth forms a flat, hard beak. Such a mouth indicates that the genus probably not only consumed small reptiles, but also insects, fruits and various forms of vegetation.

ORNITHOMIMOIDES—*Ther., Ornith., U. Cret.* This coelurosaur was discovered in southern Asia.

ORNITHOPSIS—*Saur., Brach., U. Jur. and L. Cret.* From the Isle of Wight we have the following dimensions concerning this dinosaur: dorsal vertebra, about nine inches, and cervical vertebra, about fourteen inches. The vertebrae, consisting of plates of bone, are light. This dinosaur is probably synonymous with *Pelorosaurus.* (*See* PELOROSAURUS.)

ORNITHOSUCHUS—*Ther., probably a member of a separate family, Ornithosuchidae, U. Trias. (Dasygnathoides.)* This genus, for a long time classified as an advanced thecodont, is now considered to be a primi-

Restoration of the ostrich-like dinosaur *Ornithomimus.* Courtesy of the Sinclair Oil Corporation.

tive carnosaur. Superficially, the animal was very much like a thecodont—bipedal, swift in movement, and with some armor on the back. The reptile attained a maximum length of twelve feet. *Ornithosuchus* was discovered in Scotland.

ORNITHOTARSUS—*Orn., Had., U. Cret.* From the Monmouth formation of New Jersey, this genus, apparently quite large, is known from a partial tibia, fibula, and the right third metatarsal.

ORINOSAURUS—(*See* EUSKELOSAURUS.)

OROSAURUS—(*See* EUSKELOSAURUS.)

ORTHOGONIOSAURUS—*Ther., Tyrann., U. Cret. (Indosaurus, Indosuchus.)* This carnosaur was discovered in the Lameta beds in India.

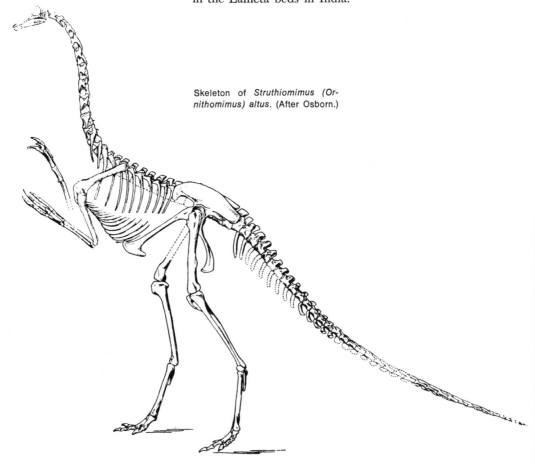

Skeleton of *Struthiomimus (Ornithomimus) altus.* (After Osborn.)

ORTHOMERUS—*Orn., Had., U. Cret. (Hecatosaurus, Limnosaurus, Telmatosaurus.)* From Holland and Transylvania, *Orthomerus* was a primitive hadrosaur with a femur almost twenty inches long and a tibia over eleven and one-half inches long. There are twelve cervical vertebrae, lacking neural spines, and these are wider than they are deep. The teeth, unlike those in most hadrosaurs, are compressed from back to front. The jugal bone is narrow.

OTOZOUM—*Trias.* The term has been given to tracks found in the Connecticut Valley. The animal that made them probably resembled *Plateosaurus.*

OVIRAPTOR—*Ther., Ornith., U. Cret.* This coelurosaur was approximately the size of a large turkey. The hard beak is toothless, implying that it subsisted on an omnivorous diet. Further implications as to the animal's food were deduced when an *Oviraptor* skeleton was discovered amid Mongolian *Protoceratops* eggs. The genus is closely related to *Ornithomimus.*

P

PACHYCEPHALOSAURUS—*Orn., Pachy., U. Cret.* The classic "bonehead" dinosaur, the brain of this genus was encased in a solid dome of bone nine inches thick. The areas toward the back of the head and above the snout was covered with a series of bumps and nodes. The reasons for such dense bone areas and the nodes are open to speculation. *Pachycephalosaurus* is the largest member of this family. It was discovered in North America.

PACHYRHINOSAURUS—*Cer., Pachyrhin., U. Cret.* From the Edmonton sediments in Alberta, Canada, this is the only known genus belonging to the family Pachyrhinosauridae, although it has been speculated that some might be found in Asia. Instead of horns, this ceratopsian had a rough boss of bone running along the top of the skull from the nose to the eyes. Ap-

Forelimb of *Struthiomimus (Ornithomimus) currellii.* (After Parks.)

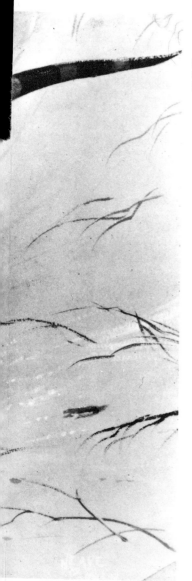

Restoration of the swift *Ornithosuchus* by Neave Parker. Courtesy of the British Museum (Natural History).

Outlined skeleton of *Ornithosuchus*. (After Newton, Broom, and Huene.)

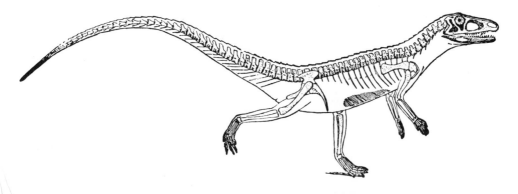

parently, *Pachyrhinosaurus* indicates a separate line of ceratopsian development.

PACHYSAURISCUS—(*See* PACHYSAURUS.)

PACHYSAUROPS—(*See* PACHYSAURUS.)

PACHYSAURUS—*Ther., U. Trias. to L. Jur. (Pachysauriscus, Pachysaurops.)* Known from fragments found in Europe, this genus is apparently closely related to *Teratosaurus*. Some paleontologists believe *Pachysaurus* to be synonymous with *Gresslyosaurus*. (*See* GRESSLYOSAURUS.)

PACHYSPONDYLUS—(*See* MASSOSPONDYLUS.)

PALAEOSAURISCUS—(*See* PALAEOSAURUS.)

Cast of brain cavity of *Indosaurus (Orthogc saurus) matleyi.* (After Huene.)

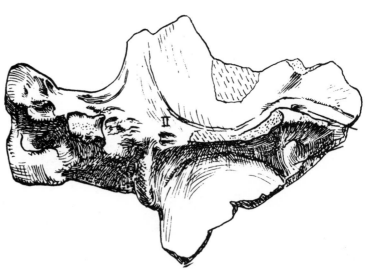

Portion of skull roof of *Indosuchus (Orthogoniosaurus) raptorius.* (After Huene.)

PALAEOSAURUS—*Ther., carnosaur of uncertain family classification, U. Trias. (Palaeosauriscus.)* This sauropod from Europe was rather heavy and approximately ten feet long. Its main weapons were strong claws, of which the fourth and fifth digits were smaller.

PALAEOSCINCUS—*Ank., Nod., U. Cret.* This fifteen-foot-long dinosaur was discovered in North America. The entire back was encased in an armored covering composed of hard plates. Along each side of the squat body and tail was a line of spikes, making this nodosaur virtually invulnerable when on its feet. Some paleontologists believe *Palaeoscincus* to be synonymous with *Edmontonia.* (*See* EDMONTONIA.)

PANOPLOSAURUS—*Ank., Nod., U. Cret.* This armored dinosaur was discovered in North America.

PARACANTHODON—*Steg. or Ank., U. Cret.* This dinosaur was discovered in South Africa. Although probably a stegosaur, some paleontologists contend that *Paracanthodon* might be an ankylosaur, possibly of the family Nodosauridae.

PARANTHODON—*Steg, Stego., L. Cret.* The genus is inadequately known, especially from a left mandible with teeth discovered in South Africa.

PARASAUROLOPHUS—*Orn., Had., U. Cret.* From the Red Deer River sediments in Alberta, Canada, this giant hadrosaur has a crest in the shape of a great tube extending from the back of the skull. This crest is formed by the premaxillary and nasal bones. Some restorations have shown a membrane attached from the crest to the back, the authenticity of which is speculative. It has been suggested that *Parasaurolophus* might actually be the male of *Kritosaurus.* (*See* KRITOSAURUS.)

PARKSOSAURUS—*Orn., Hypsil., U. Cret.* (Possibly *Thescelosaurus.*) From Alberta, Canada, the genus is known from an incomplete skeleton. The skull is incomplete yet shows that the eyes were large. The

Skull of *Limnosaurus (Orthomerus) transsylvanicus.* (After Nopcsa.)

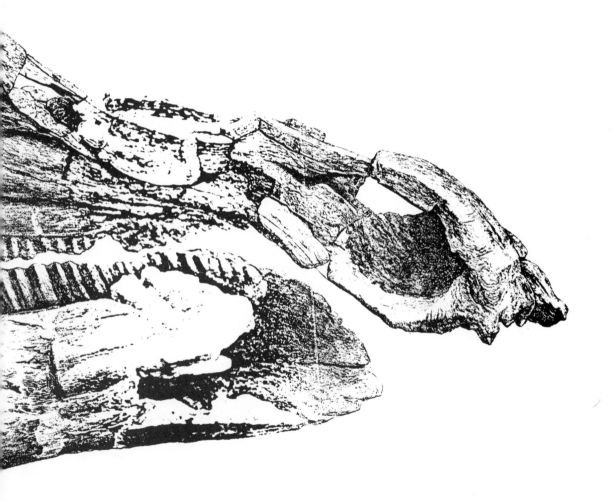

Skull of *Oviraptor philoceratops*.
(After Osborn.)

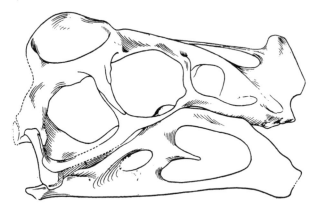

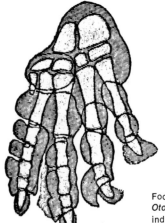

Footprints with possible bones of
Otozoum moodii. The smaller print
indicates the hand. (After Lull.)

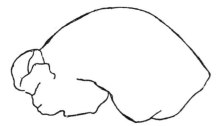

Top portion of skull of *Pachyceph-alosaurus wyomingensis.* (After Gilmore.)

Top portion of skull of *Pachyceph-alosaurus reinheimeri.* (After Brown and Schlaikjer.)

Richard S. Lull's conception of *Otozoum.* (Modified after Lull.)

animal had a long tibia, short femur, and long toes. (*See* THESCELOSAURUS.)

PARONYCHODON—*Ther., Coel., U. Cret.* This coelurosaur was discovered in North America.

PARROSAURUS—*Saur., possibly Titan., U. Cret. (Neosaurus.)* This sauropod was discovered in North America.

Skull of *Pachycephalosaurus grangeri.* Courtesy of the American Museum of Natural History.

Peishansaurus—*Ank., Nod., U. Cret.* From Ehr-chia-wu-tung in northwest China, the term has been given to a partial lower jaw, possibly that of a young form.

Restoration of the head of *Pachycephalosaurus* prepared for this book by Jim Danforth.

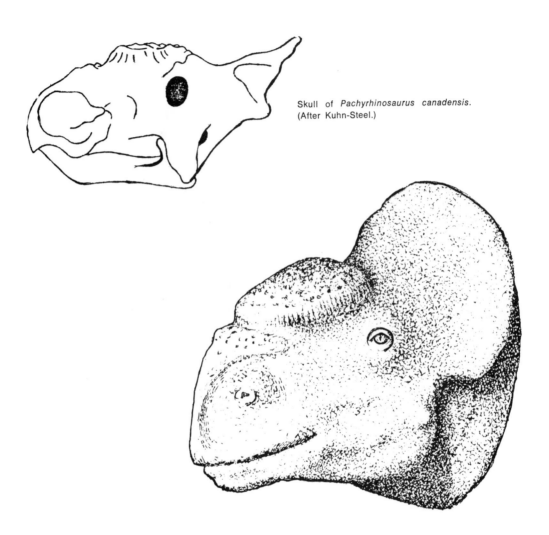

Skull of *Pachyrhinosaurus canadensis.*
(After Kuhn-Steel.)

Restoration of *Pachyrhinosaurus.*
(After Sternberg.)

Restoration of *Pachyrhinosaurus* (foreground), *Chasmosaurus* (left), and *Corytho-saurus* (right) by Neave Parker. Copyright the *Illustrated London News*.

Tooth of *Palaeosaurus (Palaeo-sauriscus) platyodon.*

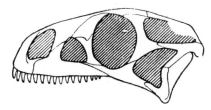

Skull of *Palaeosaurus (Palaeo-sauriscus).*

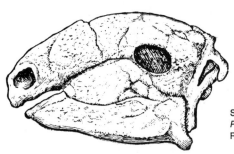

Skull of the armored dinosaur *Panoplosaurus.* (After Lambe, Romer.)

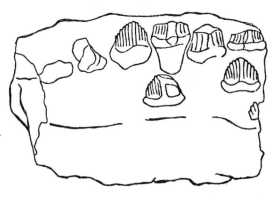

Fragmentary mandible of *Paran-thodon oweni.* (After Owen.)

Top view of skeleton of *Palaeoscincus* showing armor. Courtesy of the American Museum of Natural History.

PELOROSAURUS—*Saur., Brach., M. and U. Jur. (Caulo-don, Chondrosteosaurus, Eucamerotus, Hoplosaurus, Morinosaurus, Neosodon, Oplosaurus;* possibly *Dino-docus, Gigantosaurus, Ischyrosaurus, Ornithopsis.)* The enlarged vertebrae on the back and neck of this genus are light. *Pelorosaurus* has been found in Portugal, and in Dorset and Sussex, England. (*See* DINODOCUS, GIGANTOSAURUS, ORNITHOPSIS.)

Restoration of the armored dinosaur *Palaeoscincus*, an uninviting morsel for the Cretaceous flesh-eaters. From a mural by Charles R. Knight. Courtesy of the Field Museum of Natural History.

PELTOSAURUS—*Ank., possibly Nod., U. Cret.* The term has been temporarily given to an external skeleton with scutes. The specimen was not definitely identified by Colbert in 1962.

PENTACERATOPS—*Cer., Cerat., U. Cret.* From North America and Asia, this giant ceratopsian was named for its five "horns." Actually, the animal is three-horned, with one large horn over each eye and a smaller one above the snout. The two additional "horns" are really growths of bone extending from the region of the cheeks. The shield of *Pentaceratops* is exceptionally large.

PICRODON—(*See* GRESSLYOSAURUS.)

PINACOSAURUS—*Ank., Nod., U. Cret.* The armored dinosaur is known from fragments and incomplete skulls. The skull of *Pinacosaurus* is longer than wide and quite slender. The teeth are small, the beak rounded and without armor. The skull was protected by small plates and scutes. The remains were discovered in Mongolia and northern China.

PISANOSAURUS—*Orn., possibly a new family Pisanosauridae, M. Trias.* This primitive ornithischian is known only from fragmentary material found in Argentina, including limb bones, ribs, metatarsals and incomplete jaws.

PLATEOSAURAVUS—*Ther., Mel., U. Trias.* From the Red beds of Africa, this large prosauropod is very similar to *Plateosaurus*.

PLATEOSAURUS—*Ther., Plat., U. Trias. (Dimodosaurus, Platysaurus, Sellosaurus.)* This prosauropod from Europe was the most gigantic reptile of the Triassic Period. It was from animals such as the long-necked *Plateosaurus* that the later sauropod giants, like *Apatosaurus* and *Diplodocus*, evolved. Unlike these, however, *Plateosaurus* was mostly bipedal, occasionally coming down on all fours. Its diet may have been omnivorous. *Plateosaurus* attained an approximate length of twenty-one feet.

PLATYSAURUS—(*See* PLATEOSAURUS.)

Restoration of the crested hadrosaur *Parasaurolophus*. To the right is the theropod *Ornithomimus*. By Neave Parker.

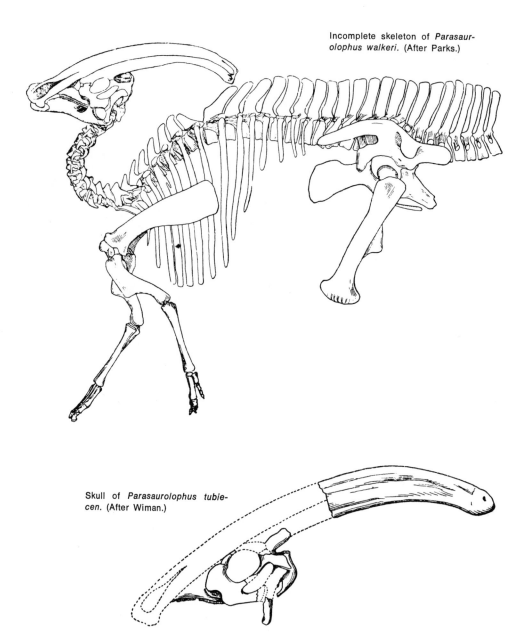

Incomplete skeleton of *Parasaur-olophus walkeri*. (After Parks.)

Skull of *Parasaurolophus tubie-cen*. (After Wiman.)

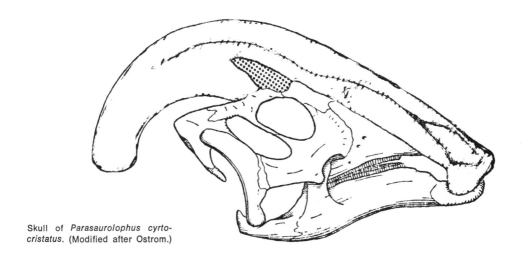

Skull of *Parasaurolophus cyrto-cristatus.* (Modified after Ostrom.)

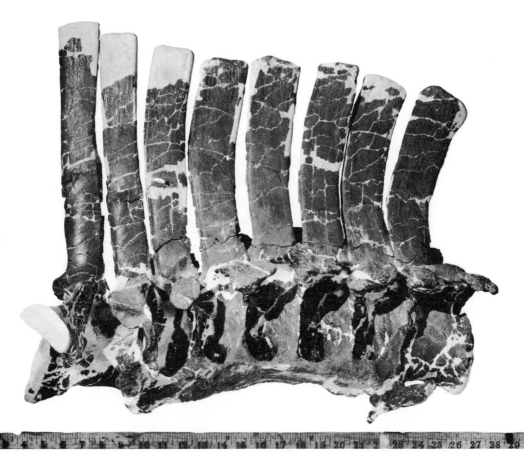

Vertebrae of *Parasaurolophus cyrtocristatus.* Courtesy of the Field Museum of Natural History.

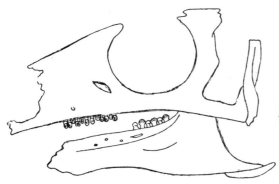

Fragmentary skull of *Parksosaurus warreni*. (After Parks.)

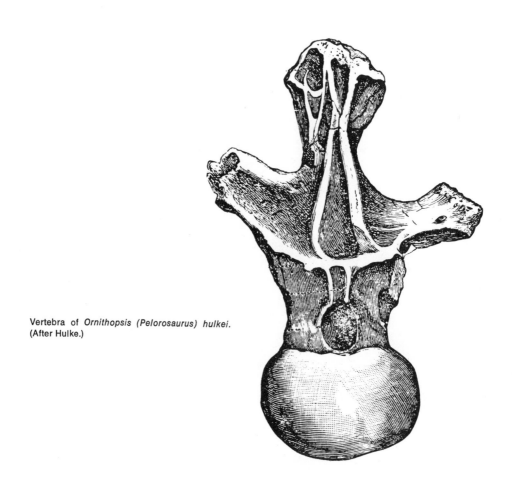

Vertebra of *Ornithopsis (Pelorosaurus) hulkei*. (After Hulke.)

Right humerus of *Pelorosaurus conybearii*. (After Owen.)

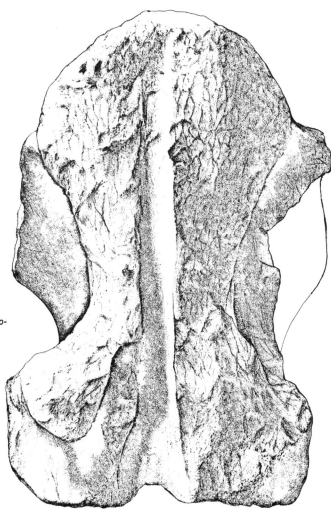

Vertebra of *Chondrosteosaurus (Pelorosaurus) gigas*. (After Owen.)

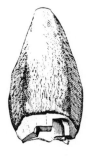

Tooth of *Hoplosaurus (Pelorosaurus) armatus*. (After Swinton.)

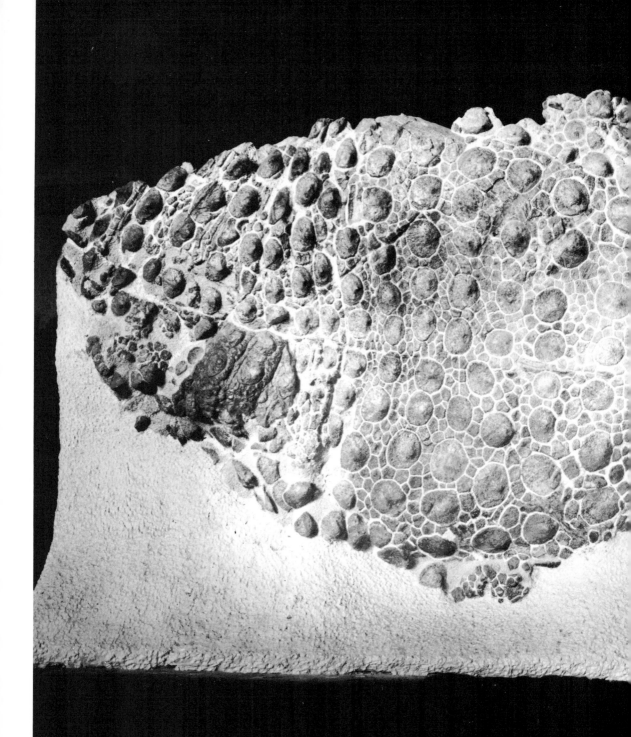

Skeleton of a nodosaur tentatively named *Peltosaurus. Courtesy* of the American Museum of Natural History.

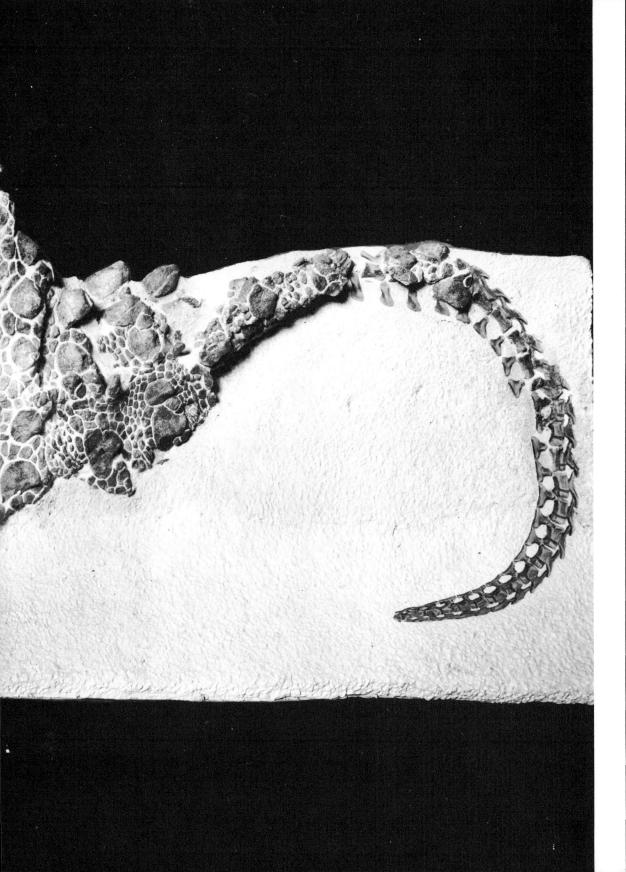

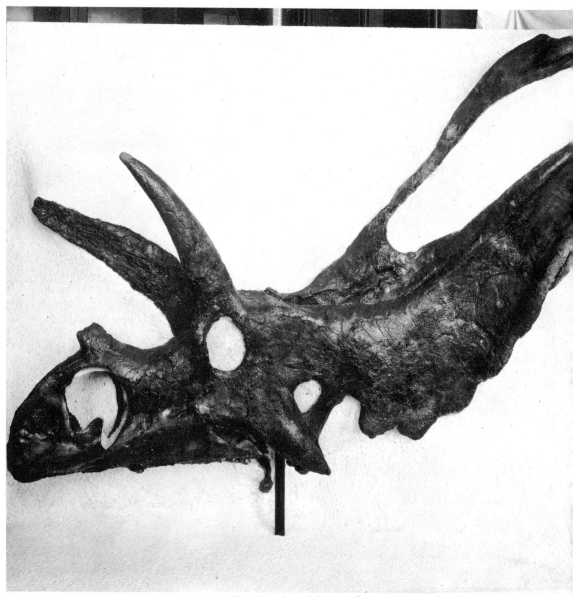

Skull of the horned dinosaur *Pentaceratops sternbergii*. Courtesy of the American Museum of Natural History.

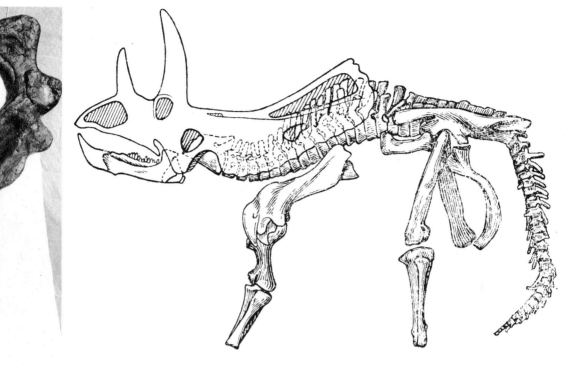

Incomplete skeleton of *Pentaceratops fenestratus*. (After Lull.)

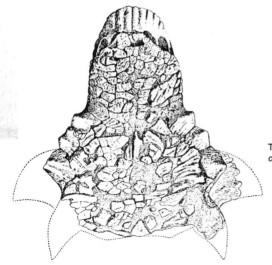

Top view of skull of the armored dinosaur *Pinacosaurus grangeri*. (After Gilmore.)

Pleurocoelis—*Saur., Brach., M. and U. Jur.* The size of a crocodile, this genus was the smallest of the American sauropods, reaching an approximate length of only thirteen feet. The skull somewhat resembles that of *Camarasaurus,* and the teeth are deep and narrow. The genus has also been found in Sussex, England. It is possible that *Pleurocoelis* is synonymous with *Astrodon.* (*See* ASTRODON.)

Pleuropeltus—(*See* STRUTHIOSAURUS.)

Pneumatoarthrus—*Cret.* The term was originally given to four vertebral centra discovered in New Jersey and believed to be hadrosaurian. Their resemblance to theropods like *Anchisaurus* and *Allosaurus* implies that they should be re-classified.

Podokesaurus—*Ther., Hall., U. Trias.* From North America, *Podokesaurus* was a small coelurosaur, only three feet in length. The animal is quite primitive, lightly built, with the general bipedal form characteristic of the Triassic theropods. *Podokesaurus* is closely related to *Coelophysis.*

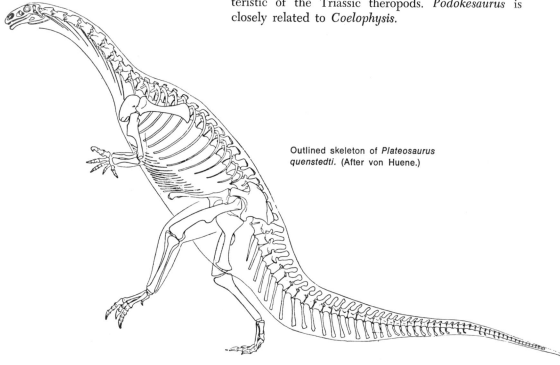

Outlined skeleton of *Plateosaurus quenstedti.* (After von Huene.)

A scene of the Upper Triassic, dominated by the giant prosauropod dinosaur *Plateosaurus* which lumbers on its hind legs while another of that genus has come down on all fours in search of food. The tiny dinosaur in the path of *Plateosaurus* is the coelurosaur *Podokesaurus*. In the foreground is the mammal-like reptile *Cynognathus* and the bipedal thecodont *Saltoposuchus*. From a mural by Rudolph F. Zallinger. Courtesy of the Peabody Museum of Natural History.

POECILOPLEURON—*Ther., Meg., M. and U. Jur. (Poicilopleuron.)* Known from fragments, this European dinosaur may be synonymous with *Allosaurus* or *Megalosaurus.* (*See* ALLOSAURUS, MEGALOSAURUS.)

POICILOPLEURON—(*See* POECILOPLEURON.)

POLACANTHOIDES—*Ank., Nod., L. Cret.* The genus is imperfectly known from a tibia and humerus found on the Isle of Wight.

Restoration of various Triassic dinosaurs, including (foreground) *Podokesaurus holyokensis,* (background) *Nanosaurus,* and (right) creatures of the *Sauropus* or *Anomoepus* type. By G. Heilmann for his book *The Origin of Birds,* published by D. Appleton-Century Company.

POLACANTHUS—*Ank., Nod., L. Cret.* This armored dinosaur from the Isle of Wight was fourteen feet long. From the neck to the hips are two rows of spikes, peaking to gigantic proportions over the shoulders. A solid shield of bone protected the hips. Following that bony mass is a double row of paired plates. Although somewhat resembling the stegosaurs, this genus is definitely a nodosaur.

POLYDONTOSAURUS—*Orn., probably Pachy., U. Cret.* This ornithopod was discovered in North America.

POLYODONTOSAURUS—(*See* TROÖDON.)

POLYONAX—*Cer., Cerat., U. Cret.* The term has been given to fragments including horn cores discovered in Colorado. The genus is usually considered synonymous with *Agathaumas mortuarius* and possibly with *Triceratops.* (*See* AGATHAUMAS, TRICERATOPS.)

POPOSAURUS—*Ther., possibly a member of a separate family, Poposauridae, U. Trias.* From North America, this carnosaur retains some of the characteristics of the ornithischians.

PRICONODON—*Steg., Stego., L. Cret.* From the Potomac formation of Maryland, this stegosaur is known only from a tooth and various fragments.

PRIODONTOGNATHUS—(*See* OMOSAURUS.)

PRIODONTOSAURUS—(*See* OMOSAURUS.)

PROCERATOPS—(*See* CERATOPS.)

PROCERATOSAURUS—*Ther., Meg.* From Gloucestershire, this dinosaur is known only from a skull over ten inches long. The reptile might be synonymous with *Megalosaurus.* (*See* MEGALOSAURUS.)

PROCHENEOSAURUS—*Orn., Had., U. Cret. (Didanodon, Tetragonosaurus.)* From the Red Deer River sediments in Alberta, Canada, this small hadrosaur has a crest in the shape of a bump, formed by the premaxillary and nasal bones. It averaged eleven feet in length, with a skull almost fourteen inches long.

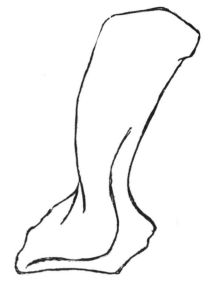

Scapula of *Polacanthoides ponderosus.* (After Nopcsa.)

Skeleton of *Polacanthus foxi.* (After Huene.)

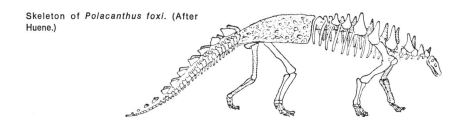

Restoration of the armored dinosaur *Polacanthus* by Neave Parker. Courtesy of the British Museum (Natural History).

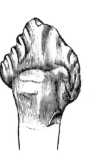

Tooth of *Pricondon crassus*.
(After Marsh.)

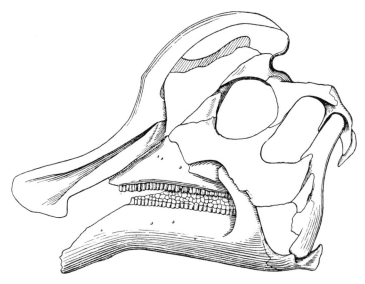

Skull of *Procheneosaurus cranibrevis*.
(After Lull-Wright.)

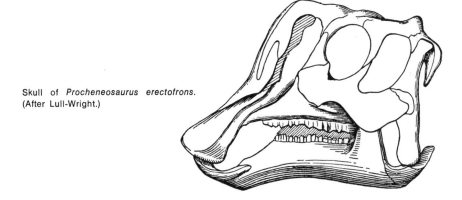

Skull of *Procheneosaurus erectofrons*.
(After Lull-Wright.)

PROCOMPSOGNATHUS—*Ther., Hall., U. Trias.* (**Possibly** *Pterospondylus.*) This coelurosaur was approximately eleven and one-half inches high at the hips. The long skull measures some three inches and is filled with curved teeth. The hind limbs are about three times the length of the forelimbs. (*See* PTEROSPONDYLUS.)

PRODEINODON—*Ther., Tyrann., U. Cret.* Known from teeth, *Prodeinodon* indicates that the giant carnosaurs were present in Mongolia's Upper Cretaceous.

PROSAUROLOPHUS—*Orn., Had., U. Cret.* From the Belly River sediments of Alberta, Canada, the animal's skull is similar to that of *Anatosaurus,* but with a low crest, formed by an extension of the nasal bones, ris-

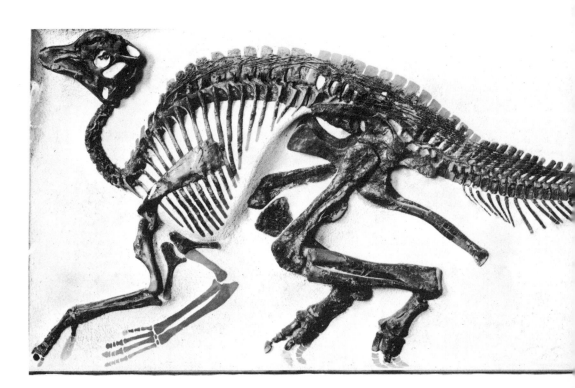

ing like knobs above the eyes. Unlike the crests of dinosaurs like *Parasaurolophus,* the crest in *Prosaurolophus* is solid, the function of which is open for speculation. It has been suggested that *Prosaurolophus* is the female form of *Saurolophus.* (*See* SAUROLOPHUS.)

PROTIGUANODON—*Cer., Psitt., L. Cret.* From Asia, this primitive ceratopsian is closely related to *Psittacosaurus.* The large ceratopsians of the Upper Cretaceous may have evolved from this genus.

PROTOCERATOPS—*Cer., Pro., U. Cret. Protoceratops* is especially significant, in that its fossil eggs were the first to be identified as those laid by a dinosaur. The

Skeleton of the duck-billed dinosaur *Procheneosaurus praeceps.* Courtesy of the American Museum of Natural History.

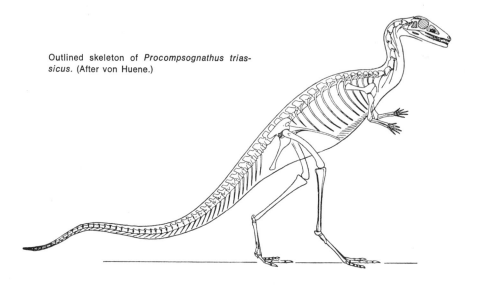

Outlined skeleton of *Procompsognathus trias-sicus.* (After von Huene.)

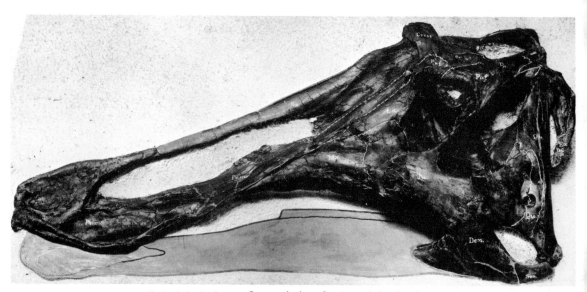

Skull of the hadrosaur *Prosaurolophus.* Courtesy of the American Museum of Natural History.

eggs and skeletons of *Protoceratops* were discovered in the Gobi Desert in 1922 by Roy Chapman Andrews. The hornless ceratopsian reached a length of only about six feet, and was a mild-looking creature when compared to the later giants of that suborder. In *Protoceratops*, however, the true ceratopsian structure is evident, thus showing a definite transitional stage in the evolution of the horned dinosaurs. The beak and shield helped to indicate what was to come.

PROTOROSAURUS—(*See* CHASMOSAURUS.)

PSITTACOSAURUS—*Cer., Psitt., L. Cret.* From Mongolia and Shantung Province, China, this reptile, classified by some paleontologists as an ornithopod, may have been a direct ancestor of the horned dinosaurs. *Psittacosaurus* was bipedal, its hind legs being about twice the length of the forelimbs. The skull, with its parrot-like beak, is of the design one would expect of a ceratopsian ancestor. The maximum length of *Psittacosaurus* was five or six feet.

Restoration of *Protiguanodon*.

Restoration of the primitive ceratopsian *Protoceratops* and its eggs. From a mural by Charles R. Knight. Courtesy of the Field Museum of Natural History.

CHAS. R. KNIGHT

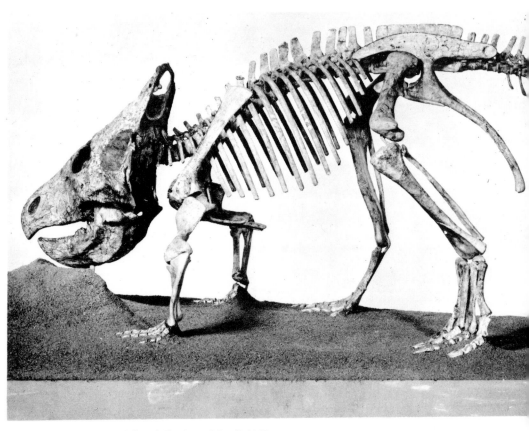

Skeleton of *Protoceratops andrewsi*. Courtesy of the Field Museum
of Natural History.

Eggs of *Protoceratops* discovered in the Gobi Desert. Courtesy of the Field Museum of Natural History.

Skull of *Psittacosaurus youngi.*
(After Kuhn-Steel.)

Skull of *Psittacosaurus sinensis.*
(After Kuhn-Steel.)

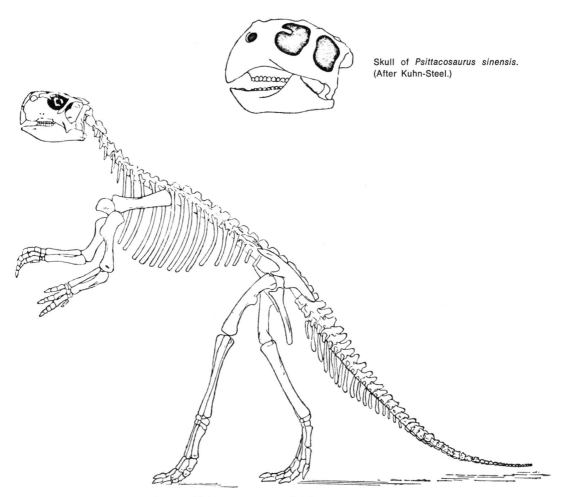

Skeleton of *Psittacosaurus mongoliensis.*
(After Osborn.)

Pteropelyx—*Orn., Had., U. Trias.* (Possibly *Thespesius, Trachodon.*) The genus is known from a partial skeleton lacking skull and teeth, discovered in the Judith River beds of Montana. It is presumed to be a flat-headed hadrosaur because of the slender ischium. *Pteropelyx* may be synonymous with *Trachodon*; and *Thespesius marginatus, T. grallipes, T. selwyni,* and *T. altidens.* (*See* THESPESIUS, TRACHODON.)

Pterospondylus—*Ther., Hall., U. Trias.* (Possibly *Procompsognathus.*) This coelurosaur was discovered in Halberstadt, Germany. (*See Procompsognathus.*)

Pterypelyx—(*See* THESPESIUS.)

Fragmentary mandible of *Psittacosaurus osborni.* (After Kuhn-Steel.)

R

Rapator—(*See* WALGETTOSUCHUS.)

Rebbachisaurus—*Saur., Titan., L. Cret.* Discovered in Africa, this genus is known from one sacrum, one humerus, one shoulder blade, and nine vertebrae. The back vertebrae are high and graceful, the last being almost five feet tall.

Regnosaurus—*Ank., Acanth., L. Cret.* Known from a lower jaw found in Europe, *Regnosaurus* may be synonomous with *Hylaeosaurus.* (*See* HYLAEOSAURUS.)

Restoration of *Psittacosaurus* (foreground) with two representatives of *Protiguanodon* to the left by Neave Parker. Courtesy of the *Illustrated London News.*

RHABDODON—*Orn., Iguan., U. Cret. (Mochlodon.)* Discovered in Europe, *Rhabdodon* is an unspecialized ornithopod not unlike *Camptosaurus.* The genus is known primarily from an incomplete skeleton of an individual slightly over sixteen feet long.

RHODANOSAURUS—*Ank., Acanth., U. Cret.* This genus from southern and central France is known imperfectly from limb bones, vertebrae, and plates and spines which served to protect the back of the creature.

RHOETOSAURUS—*Saur., Brach., L. Jur.* From Durham Downs, Queensland, Australia, *Rhoetosaurus* is one of the more ancient sauropods. It is imperfectly known from rough fragments, including the neck and back vertebrae, a femur about five feet long, portions of the pubis, and other pieces. The vertebral centrum measures approximately seven inches in length and nine and one-half inches in width.

RIGALTES—*U. Trias.* The term has been given to tracks discovered in Argentina, both front and hind feet, attributed to an ornithopod. The tracks are over three and three-fourths times as large as those of *Anchisauripus.*

S

SACROSAURUS—*Ther., Coel., L. Cret.* From England, this coelurosaur is known primarily from a small pelvis.

SALTOPUS—*Ther., Hall., U. Trias.* This coelurosaur from Europe is known primarily from an incomplete skeleton, lacking the skull, but including about fourteen dorsal vertebrae, four sacral vertebrae, and a curved femur that is shorter than the tibia. The animal probably stood some eight inches high at the hips.

SANPASAURUS—*Orn., Iguan., U. Jur.* From Weiyuan, Szechuan, China, this iguanodont is known primarily from an incomplete skeleton, which shows the femur and fibula to be relatively small and the forelimbs quite long.

Rib of *Rhabdodon priscum.*
(After Lapparent.)

Restoration of the Asian ornithopod *Sanpasaurus*, similar to *Camptosaurus*, by Neave Parker. Courtesy of the *Illustrated London News*.

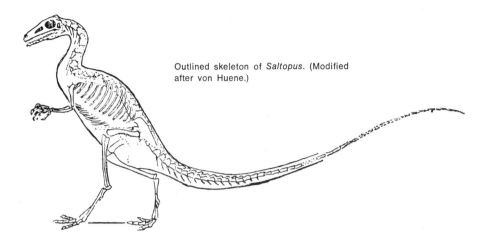

Outlined skeleton of *Saltopus*. (Modified after von Huene.)

Lower jaw of *Sarcolestes leedsi*. (After Lydekker.)

SARCOLESTES—*Steg., Scelid., U. Jur.* From the Oxford Clay of Petersborough, England, this dinosaur is known only from a partial lower jaw containing teeth. Some paleontologists believe that *Sarcolestes* is synonymous with *Scelidosaurus*, the latter, however, occurring in the Lower Jurassic.

SARCOSAURUS—*Ther., Meg., L. Jur.* This carnosaur was discovered in Europe.

SATAPLIASAURUS—*L. Cret.* The term has been given to numerous theropod tracks found in the USSR. The tracks are three-toed, with an occasional showing of a first digit. Along with these tracks were prints of almost nineteen inches long, apparently made underwater by a sauropod or ornithopod.

SAURAECHINODON—(*See* SAURECHINODON.)

SAURECHINODON—*Steg., Stego., U. Jur. (Echinodon, Sauraechinodon.)* The genus is known from fragments of jaw and teeth, similar to the teeth in *Scelidosaurus*, found at Durlston Bay, Dorsetshire, England.

Footprints of *Satapliasaurus*. From left to right, *S. tchaboukanii, S. dzotsenidzei, S. kandelakii,* and a print possibly made by an ornithopod. (After Gabouniia.)

Saurolophus—*Orn., Had., U. Cret.* From the Edmonton beds of Alberta, Canada, and from Asia, the animal's skull has a spike-like crest, formed by an extension of the nasal bones rising high over the head. Unlike the air storage crests of dinosaurs such as *Lambeosaurus,* the crest in *Saurolophus* is solid, its function indeterminate. It has been speculated that this dinosaur might be the male form of *Prosaurolophus.* (*See* PROSAUROLOPHUS.)

Saurophagus—(*See* ALLOSAURUS.)

Sauroplites—*Ank., Nod., L. Cret.* From Tebch, northwest China, this armored dinosaur is known from fragments including plates, ribs, and an incomplete ischium.

Sauropus—*Trias.* The term has been given to tracks found in the Connecticut Valley, apparently made by a dinosaur similar to *Hypsilophodon,* but with hands like *Camptosaurus.* The animal was seemingly capable of some quadrupedal locomotion.

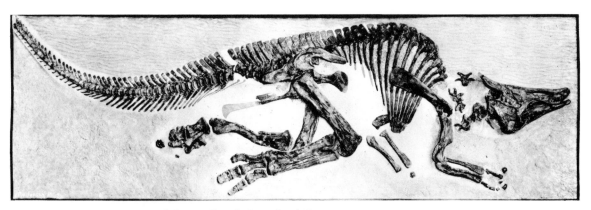

Skeleton of the duck-billed dinosaur *Saurolophus osborni.* Courtesy of the American Museum of Natural History.

Skull of *Saurolophus angustirostris.*

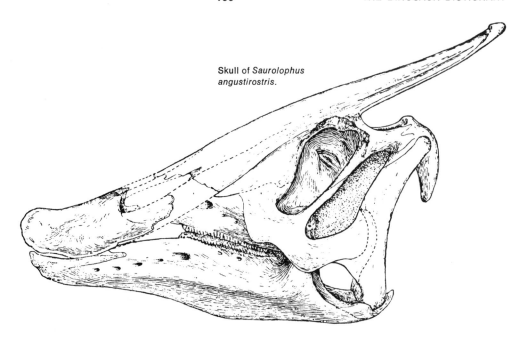

Restoration of the duck-billed dinosaur *Saurolophus* by Neave Parker. Courtesy of the *Illustrated London News.*

SAURORNITHOIDES—*Ther., Coel., U. Cret.* This genus from eastern Asia has a skull over six and one-half inches long.

SCELIDOSAURUS—*Steg., Scel., L. Jur.* (*Possibly Sarcolestes.*) The oldest known ornithischian and the first of the plated dinosaurs, this genus was about twelve feet long. The basic form of this dinosaur is typically stegosaurian—the hind legs are longer than the forelimbs—yet the animal was still quadrupedal, with broad feet. The small skull contains weak jaws and the body was heavy and protected by armor plating. These plates ran in rows from the neck down along the back and tail. Vertical plates stood upright along the top of the neck and tail. (*See* SARCOLESTES.)

SCLERMOCHLUS—*Ther., Hall., U. Trias.* This small genus, long classified as an advanced thecodont, is now considered to be a primitive carnosaur. In appearance, the animal greatly resembled its thecodont predecessors. *Sclermochlus* was discovered in northeastern Scotland.

SCOLOSAURUS—*Ank., Nod., U. Cret.* The neck of this North American armored genus was protected by large, strong plates. The back armor is formed in segments. Pointed ridges protrude from the body at various places. The heavy tail is armed with two large spikes. *Scolosaurus* attained a length of approximately thirteen feet and a width of over five and one-half feet.

SEGISAURUS—*Ther., Seg., L. Jur.* This light-weight coelurosaur from Arizona is known primarily from a left shoulder blade and a collar bone which are almost complete. The bones are similar to those of *Compsognathus,* only larger. The hand resembles those of *Compsognathus, Ornithomimus,* and *Ornitholestes.*

SELENICHNUS—*Trias.* The term has been given to dinosaur tracks discovered in the Connecticut Valley. Apparently, the animal that made the tracks was bipedal, perhaps a coelurosaur resembling *Saltopus.*

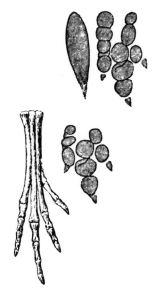

Footprints of *Sauropus barrattii* and possible bones. (After Lull.)

Richard S. Lull's conception of *Sauropus.* (Modified after Lull.)

SELLOSAURUS—(*See* PLATEOSAURUS.)

SILVASAURUS—*Ank., Nod., U. Cret.* From Kansas, this armored dinosaur is known from a skull and an incomplete skeleton. The head, one fourth longer than wide, is broader toward the rear and is at the end of a relatively long neck. This primitive ankylosaur was armed with plates, and the tail and body were protected by spikes running along the sides. The creature attained an approximate length of over ten and one-half feet.

SINOCOELRUS—*Ther., Coel., U. Jur.* This coelurosaur was discovered in eastern Asia.

SMILODON—(*See* CLADEIODON.)

SPHENOSPONDYLUS—(*See* IGUANODON.)

SPINOSAURUS—*Ther., Meg., U. Cret.* From Egypt, this genus is distinguished by enormous back spines, some of which attained a length of six feet. The superficial effect produced by the spines is a bipedal dinosaur version of such Permian fin-backed pelyco-

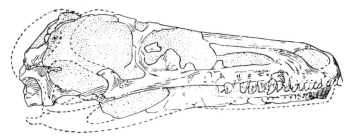

Skull of *Saurornithoides mongoliensis.*
(After Osborn.)

saurs as *Dimetrodon* and *Edaphosaurus*. The reasons for this spine-backed phenomenon are open to speculation. Another characteristic of *Spinosaurus* is that the teeth are straight, not curved, in the back.

SPINOSUCHUS—*Ther., probably Hall., U. Trias.* This coelurosaur was discovered in North America.

SPONDYLOSOMA—*Ther., Theco., U. Trias.* This prosauropod was discovered in South America.

STEGOCERAS—*Orn., Pachy., U. Cret. ("Troödon.")* From North America and Asia, this ornithopod had not yet attained the grotesque appearance of *Pachycephalosaurus. Stegoceras* was a modest sized dinosaur of this family, approximately six feet in length.

STEGOPELTA—*Ank, Nod., U. Cret.* This armored dinosaur from Wyoming is known from incomplete upper and lower jaws, plus numerous fragments including scutes, large plates, and spines. The area of the hips was protected by plates. The neck was shielded by similar armor. The front section of the body has smaller armor in the form of random scutes. A heavy club of bone, similar to that in some of the Cenozoic glyptodonts, is at the end of the tail and was probably used as a weapon. The head is relatively small.

STEGOSAURIDES—*Ank., Nod., U. Cret.* From Hui-hui-p'u, northwest China, this armored dinosaur is known only from fragments, including the base of a dermal spine and two vertebrae.

STEGOSAUROIDES—*Ank., probably Nod., U. Cret. (Stegosaurides.)* This armored dinosaur was discovered in North America and eastern Asia.

SREGOSAURUS—*Steg., Stego., U. Jur. (Hypsirhophus, Hysirophus;* possibly *Diracodon.)* This odd-looking North American dinosaur, twenty-five feet long and weighing four tons, managed some very meager protection from the two rows of alternating triangular plates running along the neck, back, and tail. Its real

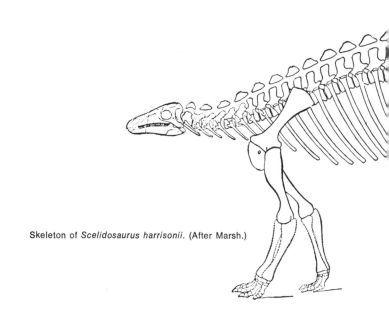

Skeleton of *Scelidosaurus harrisonii*. (After Marsh.)

Restoration of the primitive stegosaur *Scelido-saurus* by Neave Parker. Courtesy of the British Museum (Natural History).

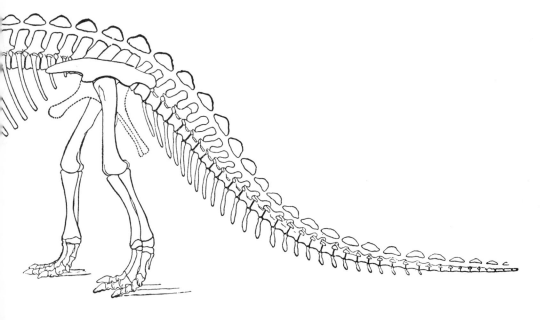

Restoration of the primitive theropod *Schlermochlus* by Neave
Parker. Courtesy of the British Museum (Natural History).

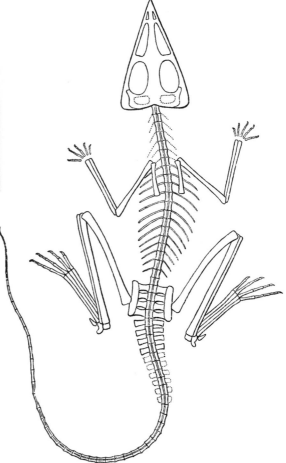

Skeleton of *Schlermochlus taylori.*

defense came from four tail spikes that could smash into the Jurassic theropods with telling impact. The animal is perhaps most famous for its supposed three "brains," two of which were actually enlargements of the spinal cord in the shoulder and pelvic regions. These enlargements, much larger than the actual brain, controlled the movements of the legs and tail. This arrangement was not uncommon among the dinosaurs. (*See* DIRACODON.)

STENONYCHOSAURUS—*Ther., U. Cret.* This theropod of uncertain classification was discovered in North America.

STENOPELIX—*Orn., Psitt., L. Cret.* From Bückeburg in Northern Germany, the genus is known imperfectly

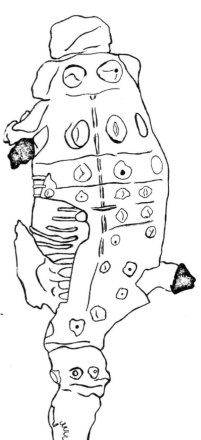

Partial skeleton of *Scolosaurus cutleri.* (After Kuhn-Steel.)

Restoration of the armored dinosaur *Scolosaurus* by A. S. Woodward.

Skull of the armored dinosaur *Silva-saurus condrayi*. (After Kuhn-Steel.)

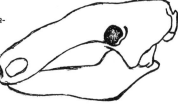

Forelimb of the theropod dinosaur *Segisaurus halli*. (After Camp.)

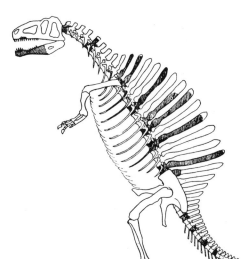

Skeleton of the African theropod *Spino-saurus aegypticus*. (After Lapparent.)

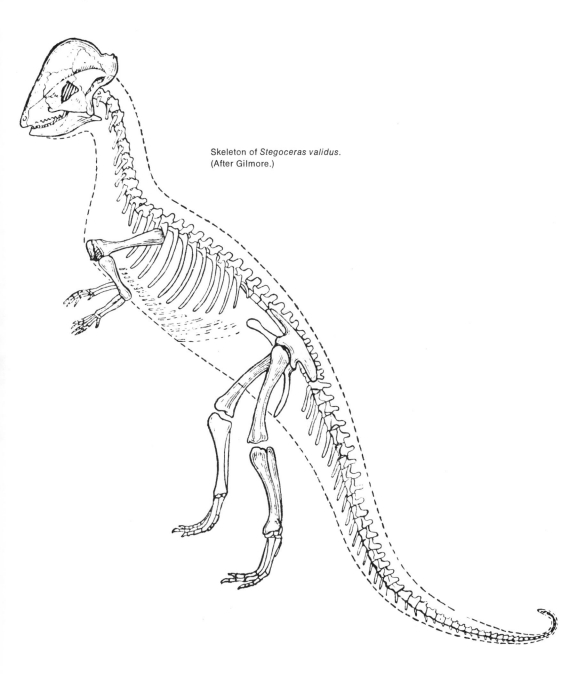

Skeleton of *Stegoceras validus*.
(After Gilmore.)

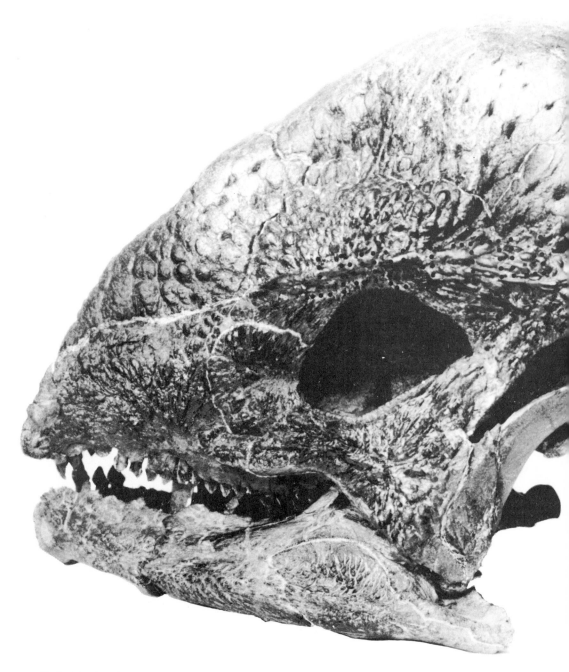

Skull of the bone-head ornithopod *Stegoceras validus*. Courtesy of the Smithsonian Institution.

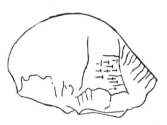

Top of skull of *Stegoceras lambei.*
(After Sternberg.)

Top of skull of *Stegoceras edmon-
tonensis.* (After Brown and Schlaikjer.)

Top of skull of *Stegoceras stern-
bergi.* (After Brown and Schlaikjer.)

Skeleton of *Stegosaurus stenops*. Courtesy of the Smithsonian Institution.

from material including vertebrae, the left hind limb, and a partial pelvic girdle. It has been theorized that *Stenopelix* is related to *Hypsilophodon.*

STEPHANOSAURUS—(*See* LAMBEOSAURUS.)

STEREOCEPHALUS—(*See* ANKYLOSAURUS.)

STERRHOLOPHUS—*Cer., Cerat., U. Cret.* (**Possibly *Triceratops.***) The term has been given to an immature ceratopsian skull, usually considered synonymous with *Triceratops flabellatus.* The separate genus was given by Marsh who stated that, unlike *Triceratops,* the back of the crest was not free and horny, but covered with strong muscles and ligaments that helped support the heavy skull. The bones above the eyes stand up straight and curve·forward at the tips. (*See* TRICERATOPS.)

"STREPTOSPONDYLUS"—(*See* EUSTREPTOSPONDYLUS.)

STRUTHIOMIMUS—(*See* ORNITHOMIMUS.)

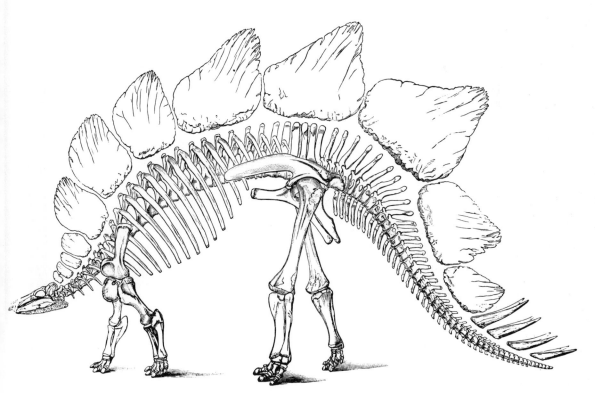

Early restoration of the skeleton of *Stegosaurus ungulatus* incorrectly showing the plates arranged in pairs and eight tail spikes. (After Marsh.)

Restoration of the plated dinosaur *Stegosaurus* in its Jurassic environment. From a mural by Charles R. Knight. Courtesy of the Field Museum of Natural History.

Struthiosaurus—*Ank., Acanth., U. Cret. (Crataeomus, Danubriosaurus, Pleuropeltus.)* From Europe, this dinosaur is primarily known from a partial birdlike skull, various pieces of armor, plates, and large spines. Early restorations showed the genus resembling *Polacanthus.*

Styracosaurus—*Cer., Cerat., U. Cret.* This dinosaur was a short-frilled ceratopsian, endowed with a number of long shield spikes. Extremely short horns are above the snout. The creature attained a length of about eighteen feet. *Styracosaurus* was discovered in Alberta, Canada.

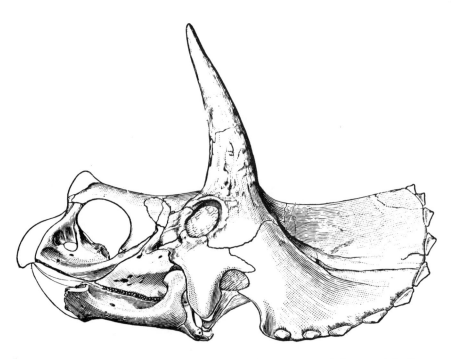

Skull of *Sterrholophus flabellatus,* a horned dinosaur of the Upper Cretaceous. (After Marsh.)

Succinodon—*Saur., Titan., U. Cret.* This sauropod was discovered in Europe.

Symphyrophus—*Saur., U. Jur.* This sauropod of uncertain classification was discovered in North America.

Syngonosaurus—*Orn., Iguan., U. Cret.* (**Possibly** *Anoplosaurus.*) The dinosaur is known from fragments, including nineteen incomplete vertebrae and other material possibly applicable, found in England. (*See* anoplosaurus.)

Syrmosaurus—*Ank., Nod., L. Cret.* From Mongolia, this primitive ankylosaur was armed with symmetrical

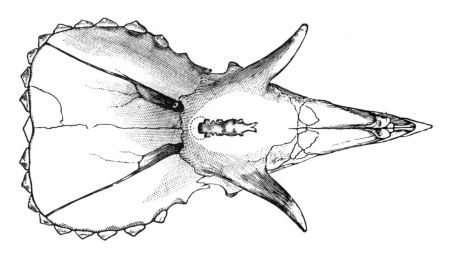

Top view of skull of *Sterrholophus flabellatus.* (After Marsh.)

Incomplete lower jaw of *Struthiosaurus austriacus*. (After Nopcsa.)

Rear view of skull of *Struthiosaurus transsylvanicus*. (After Nopcsa.)

Hypothetical restoration of *Struthiosaurus*. (Based on an early model.)

Skull of *Styracosaurus albertensis*. Courtesy of the Geological Survey of Canada.

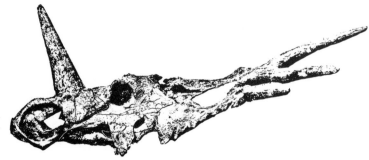

rows of pointed plates. These plates, separated and not joined together into a single mass, protected the neck, back, limbs and tail. A heavy, solid club at the end of the long tail served as a defensive weapon. This squat reptile varied in length from twelve to fifteen feet.

SZECHUSANOSAURUS—*Ther., possibly Tyrann., U. Cret.* This carnosaur was discovered in eastern Asia.

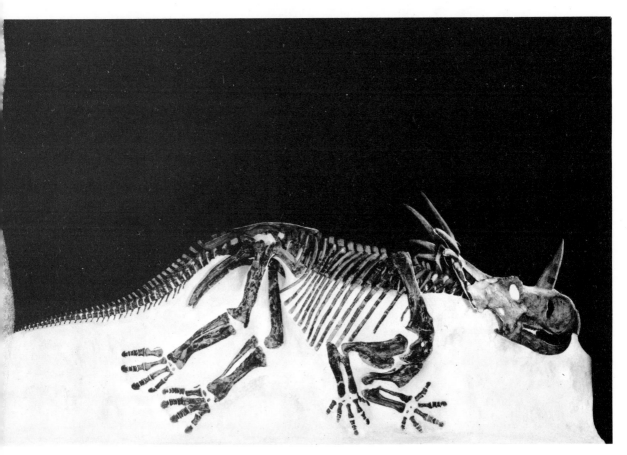

Skeleton of *Styracosaurus parks.* Courtesy of the American Museum of Natural History.

Model of *Styracosaurus* by C. W. Gilmore. Courtesy of the Smithsonian Institution.

T

TALARURUS—*Ank., Nod., U. Cret.* From Bain Chiri, Mongolia, this armored dinosaur is known from the back portion of the skeleton which is not complete. Keeled plates almost two inches thick protected the back, hips, and tail. The sides of the body and tail

Restoration of the theropod *Szechuanosaurus* by Neave Parker. Courtesy of the *Illustrated London News*.

were armed with sharp spines. The skull when complete was probably narrow. In life the reptile was about seventeen feet long. *Talarurus* is probably closely related to *Euoplocephalus.*

TANIUS—*Orn., Had., U. Cret.* From Shantung, China, this duckbilled dinosaur is known from an incomplete skeleton. The skull lacks the anterior portion but implies that *Tanius* had a flat, low head and is closely allied with *Anatosaurus.*

Restoration of the duck-billed dinosaur *Tanius* by Neave Parker. Courtesy of the *Illustrated London News.*

TARBOSAURUS—*Ther., Tyrann., U. Cret.* From eastern
Asia, this genus is of the general tyrannosaurid form.
The animal was approximately twenty-three feet long,
almost ten feet high at the hips, with a skull almost
four feet long and a hand five and one-half inches
long. Each hand was probably equipped with two
claws.

TATISAURUS—*Orn., Hypsil. or a separate family Heterodontosauridae, U. Trias.* From eastern Asia, this prim-

Restoration of the duck-billed dinosaur *Thespesius* by Charles R. Knight.

Caudal vertebra of *Thespesius occidentalis.* (After Leidy.)

itive ornithopod is known from a partial left mandible with teeth resembling those of the thecodonts.

TEINUROSAURUS—(*See* GORGOSAURUS.)

TELMATOSAURUS—(*See* ORTHOMERUS.)

TERATOSAURUS—*Ther., Ter., U. Trias.* Unlike its coelurosaur contemporaries, *Teratosaurus* was a large and heavy theropod, some fifty feet long, with a weight of more than half a ton. The forelimbs, about a third shorter than the hind legs, have three-fingered hands equipped with great claws. The neck was short and muscular. The head is large and the mouth filled

Skeleton of a hadrosaur first labeled as *Trachodon mirabilis* but now considered to be *Anatosaurus annectens* or more correctly *Thespesius occidentalis.* Courtesy of the South Dakota School of Mines and Technology.

Restoration of the armored dinosaur *Syrmosaurus*. (After Maleev.)

Tail of *Syrmosaurus viminicaudus*.
(After Maleev.)

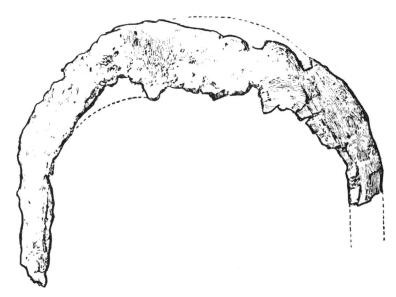

Bone of the ankylosaur *Talarurus plicatospineus*. (After Maleev.)

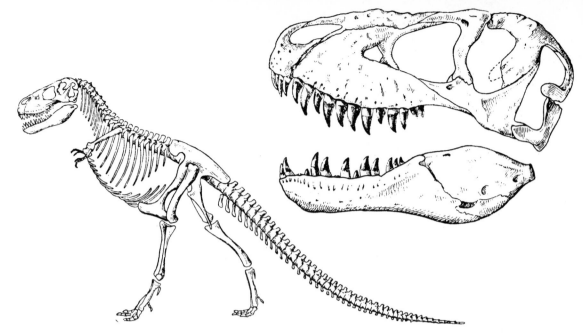

Skeleton and skull of the theropod dinosaur *Tarbosaurus efremovi*. (After Maleev.)

Mandible of *Tatisaurus oebleri*. (After Simmons.)

Skull of *Teratosaurus*. (After Huene.)

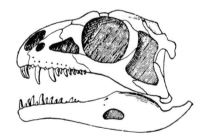

with formidable teeth. This early carnosaur established a trend later fulfilled by the giant flesh-eaters of the Cretaceous Period.

TETRAGONOSAURUS—*Orn., Had., U. Cret.* From the Belly River formation in Alberta, Canada, this dinosaur is probably synonymous with *Procheneosaurus*. (*See* PROCHENEOSAURUS.)

TETRAPODOSAURUS—*L. Cret.* The term has been given to tracks found in the Peace River area of Canada. The prints are both four- and five-toed, indicating a quadrupedal animal, the classification of which has not yet been determined.

THECOCOELURUS—*Ther., Coel., L. Cret.* This European carnosaur is considered by some paleontologists to be synonymous with *Thecospondylus*. (*See* THECOSPONDYLUS.)

THECODONTOSAURUS—*Ther., Theco., U. Trias.* From North America, Asia, Africa, and Europe, this genus was named for its similarities to the thecodonts. The teeth are serrated and leaf-shaped. The genus is considered to be even more primitive than the giant *Plateosaurus*.

Tooth of the prosauropod dinosaur *Thecodontosaurus platyodon.*

Restoration of the Triassic theropod dinosaur *Teratosaurus.*

THECOSPONDYLUS—*Ther., Coel., L. Cret.* Known from fragments found in Europe, this coelurosaur is closely related to *Elaphrosaurus*. Some paleontologists believe *Thecospondylus* to be synonymous with *Thecocoelurus*.

THEROSAURUS—(*See* IGUANODON.)

THESCELOSAURUS—*Orn., Hyps., U. Cret.* From western Canada, this slender, swift-moving ornithopod, approximately eight feet long, is related to *Camptosaurus*.

Skeleton of *Thescelosaurus neglectus.* Courtesy of the Smithsonian Institution.

Model of the herbivorous dinosaur *Thescelosaurus* by C. W. Gilmore. Courtesy of the Smithsonian Institution.

THESPESIUS—*Orn., Had., U. Cret.* From the Great Lignite formation, Grand River, South Dakota, this genus is known from inadequate specimens, including a partial skull and other incomplete material. This genus may be synonymous with *Cionodon, Diclonius,* and *Pteropelyx (Trachodon).* (*See* CIONODON, DICLONIUS, PTEROPELYX, TRACHODON.)

TICHOSTEUS—*Ther., U. Jur.* This theropod of uncertain classification was discovered in North America.

TIENSHANOSAURUS—*Saur., Brach., L. Cret.* This sauropod was discovered in eastern Asia.

Titanosaurus—*Saur., Titan., U. Cret.* From South America, Europe, and Asia, *Titanosaurus*, despite its name, was actually a relatively small sauropod. The genus is known by many types and closely related genera.

Tornieria—*Saur., Titan., U. Jur. (Gigantosaurus.)* From East Africa, this large genus is known from a tibia two and one-half feet long, a femur of four and one-

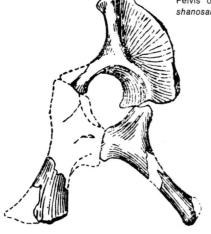

Pelvis of the sauropod dinosaur *Tienshanosaurus*. (After Young.)

Incomplete left radius of *Titanosaurus indicus*. (After Huene.)

half feet, a humerus seven feet long, and some metatarsals from almost four to more than six inches in
length. The forelegs are about the same length as the
hind legs. The height at the shoulder was probably
some twenty feet.

TOROSAURUS—*Cer., Cerat., U. Cret.* From the Laramie
formation of Wyoming, this genus has the longest
skull of any terrestrial animal—eight feet long, includ-

Restoration of the sauropod dinosaur *Titanosaurus* by G. Biese under
the direction of von Huene.

ing the enormous shield—with two exceptionally large horns above the eyes and a small horn over the snout. This genus shows the termination of ceratopsian development, appearing even after the less specialized *Triceratops*, making this one of the last dinosaurs.

TRACHODON—*Orn., Had., U. Cret. (Anatosaurus; possibly Kritosaurus, Pteropelyx, Thespesius.)* The genus was first established for a fossil hadrosaurian tooth

Tooth of *"Trachodon" cantabrigiensis*. (After Lydekker.)

Skull and model of the giant ceratopsian dinosaur *Torosaurus*. Courtesy of the Academy of Natural Sciences.

discovered in Montana. This dinosaur is usually re-
garded as synonymous with *Anatosaurus. Trachodon
breviceps,* known from a dental battery, is considered
synonymous with *Kritosaurus.* (*See* ANATOSAURUS, KRI-
TOSAURUS, PTEROPELYX, THESPESIUS.)

TRIASSOLESTES—*Ther., Hall., possibly M. Trias.* This
coelurosaur was discovered in South America.

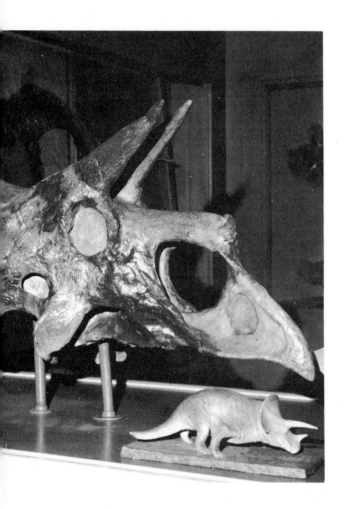

Triceratops—*Cer., Cerat., U. Cret.* (Possibly *Agathaumas, Polyonax, Sterrholophus.*) From North America, this was one of the largest of the ceratopsians, culminating the evolution of that suborder. The animal was some thirty feet long, with a weight of seven tons. The skull alone measured seven feet long. *Triceratops* was a fierce-looking herbivore, with a short, solid frill, and three horns, two long ones over the

eyes and one short horn over the snout. *Triceratops* was indeed well fortified against the monstrous carnosaurs of the Cretaceous Period. The creature was probably one of the last dinosaurs to meet extinction. (*See* AGATHAUMAS, POLYONAX, STERRHOLOPHUS.)

"TROÖDON"—*Ther., Coel., U. Cret.* (*Polydontosaurus.*) This coelurosaur was discovered in North America.

Restoration of *Torosaurus* by Neave Parker. Courtesy of the *Illustrated London News.*

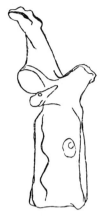

First cervical vertebra of *Tricera-tops maximus*. (After Kuhn-Steel.)

"Troödon"—*Orn., Pachy., U. Cret.* (*See* STEGOCERAS.)

Tsintaosaurus—*Orn., Had, U. Cret.* (Possibly *Tanius.*) From Shantung, China, this recently discovered dinosaur has a solid crest in the shape of a verticle blade above the eyes, which is formed by an extension of the nasal bones. (*See* TANIUS.)

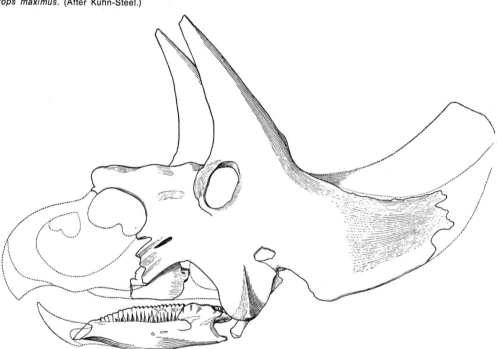

Skull of *Triceratops obtusis*. (After Lull.)

TYRANNOSAURUS—*Ther., Tyrann., U. Cret. (Dynamo-saurus; probably Manospondylus).* The largest and most highly evolved of all theropods, *Tyrannosaurus* was the most powerful animal ever to walk this planet. This carnosaur stood eighteen feet high, with a length of fifty feet. The head was enormous, supported by the eight-ton weight of the brute, with dagger-like teeth

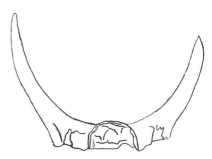

Horn cores of *Triceratops alticornis.* (After Kuhn-Steel.)

Skull of *Triceratops horridus.* Courtesy of the South Dakota School of Mines and Technology.

Skeleton of *Triceratops prorsus*. Courtesy of the Smithsonian Institution.

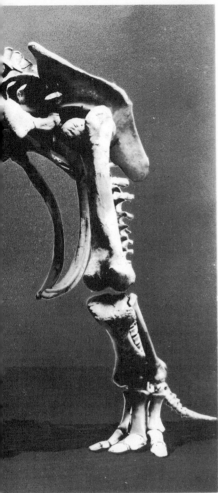

Skull of *Triceratops calicornis*. Courtesy of the Field Museum of Natural History.

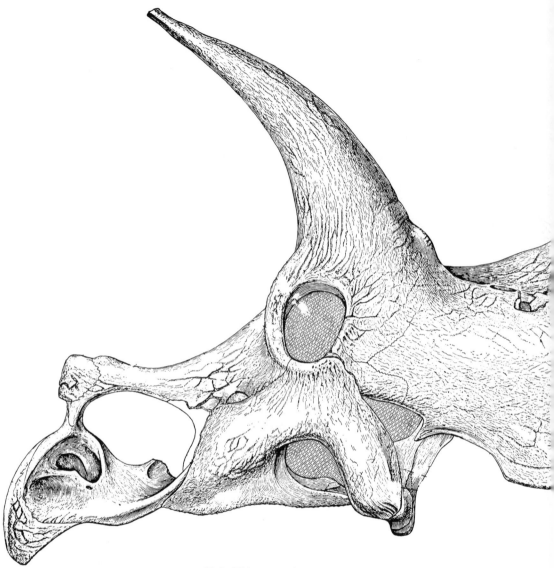

Skull of *Triceratops elatus*.
(After Marsh.)

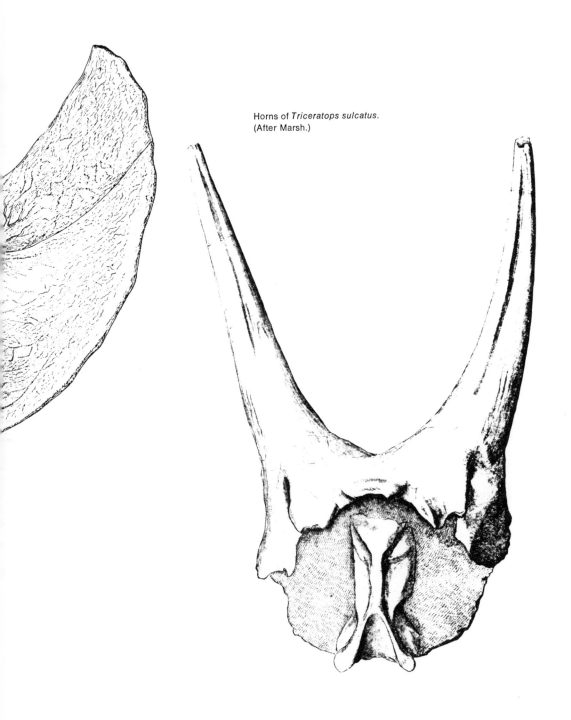

Horns of *Triceratops sulcatus*.
(After Marsh.)

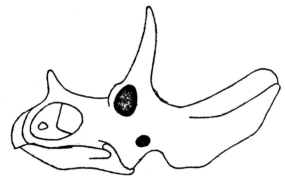

Skull of *Triceratops albertensis.* (After Kuhn-Steel.)

Nasal horn of *Triceratops galeus.* (After Kuhn-Steel.)

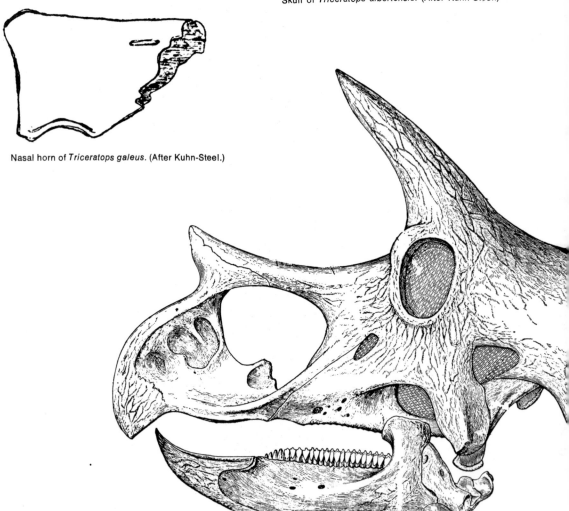

Skull of *Triceratops brevicornis.*
(After Marsh.)

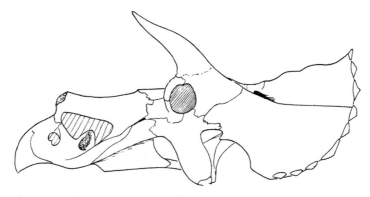

Skull of *Triceratops serratus.*
(After Huene.)

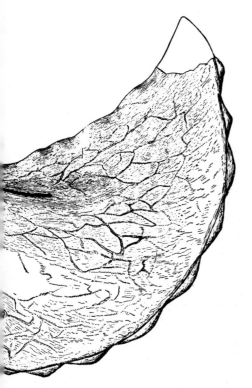

Skull of *Triceratops eurycephalus.* (After Kuhn-Steel.)

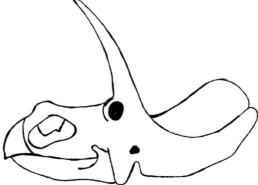

The hadrosaur *Tsintaosaurus* watches gliding *Pteranodons*. Scene from the film *Dinosaurs: The Terrible Lizards*. Copyright 1970 by Wah Chang.

Model of the great horned dinosaur *Triceratops elatus* by C. W. Gilmore. Courtesy of the Smithsonian Institution.

from three to six inches in length. The forelimbs are reduced to ridiculous, useless appendages, each with two claws. It is not unlikely that, due to the mass and high degree of specialization, *Tyrannosaurus* was only able to pursue the slow-moving armored or horned dinosaurs, finding food more readily available as a scavenger. *Tyrannosaurus* was discovered in North America and eastern Asia.

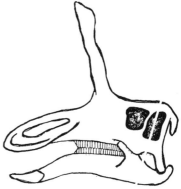

Skull of the duck-billed dinosaur *Tsintaosaurus spinorhinus*. (After Kuhn-Steel.)

U

UINTASAURUS—*Saur., Brach., M. and U. Jur.* Known primarily from vertebrae discovered in the Morrison formation of Utah, it apparently had a relatively short

Skeleton of theropod dinosaur *Dynamosaurus (Tyrannosaurus) imperiosus.* Courtesy of the British Museum (Natural History).

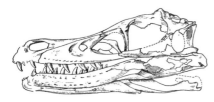

Skull of the theropod dinosaur *Velociraptor mongoliensis*. (After Osborn.)

neck. The estimated length of this dinosaur is from almost forty-nine to fifty-two and one-half feet. Some paleontologists believe *Uintasaurus* to be synonymous with *Camarasaurus*. (*See* CAMARASAURUS.)

V

VECTISAURUS—*Orn., Iguan., L. Cret.* From the Isle of Wight, the genus is known from incomplete material, including six large vertebrae and a partial ilium. A skull fragment not unlike *Stegoceras* might apply to *Vectisaurus*.

VELOCIPES—*Ther., Hall., U. Trias.* This coelurosaur was discovered in Europe.

VELOCIRAPTOR—*Ther., Coel., U. Cret.* From Mongolia, this small, lightweight coelurosaur has some megalosaurian characteristics. The head is lengthened to

The classic dinosaur confrontation of the Cretaceous Period: the flesh-eating *Tyrannosaurus* vs. the three-horned *Triceratops*. From a mural by Charles R. Knight. Courtesy of the Field Museum of Natural History.

forty-two inches, with large eyes, and teeth running to the rear of the mouth.

VIMINICAUDUS—*Ank., Nod., U. Cret.* This armored dinosaur was discovered in eastern Asia.

W

WALGETTOSUCHUS—*Ther., possibly Coel., L. Cret.* (**Probably** *Fulgurotherium, Rapator.*) This coelurosaur was discovered in Australia.

Y

YALEOSAURUS—*Ther., Theco, U. Trias.* (**Probably** *Amphisaurus, Anchisaurus, Megadactylus.*) The term was given to *Anchisaurus colurus* by von Huene, who had studied the prosauropod and felt the new classi-

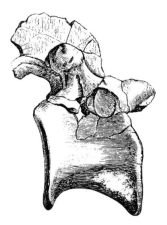

Bone of *Zanclodon laevis*.

fication valid. The validity, however, is open to discussion. (*See* ANCHISAURUS.)

YAXARTOSAURUS—(*See* JAXARTOSAURUS.)

YUNNANOSAURUS—*Ther., Plat., U. Trias.* From Asia, this genus, similar to *Massospondylus,* is known from some twenty individuals. A similar skeleton has been found in Arizona, and three linked vertebrae in India.

Z

ZANCLODON—*Ther., possibly Mel., Trias.* The teeth of this dinosaur are smooth, the edges being serrated or whole. The neural spines are high and broad.

ZAPSALIS—*Ther., U. Cret.* This theropod of uncertain classification was discovered in North America.

ZATOMUS—*Probably Ther., U. Trias.* This dinosaur was discovered in North America.

Skeleton of the theropod *Tyrannosaurus rex,* incorrectly showing three claws on the hand. Courtesy of the American Museum of Natural History.

Limb bone of *Zanclodon*.

Bibliography

The amount of reference material pertaining to dinosaurs is virtually unlimited. The sources from which I obtained the most significant and valuable information, and to whose authors I give sincere thanks, are listed as follows:

Colbert, Edwin H., *Dinosaurs—Their Discovery and Their World*, E. P. Dutton & Co., New York, 1961. (The outlining of Saurischia and Ornithischia in this book was based upon Dr. Colbert's breakdown.)

De Camp, L. Sprague, and De Camp, Catherine Crook, *The Day of the Dinosaur*, Doubleday & Co., Garden City, New York, 1968.

Gilmore, C. W., "Osteology of the armored Dinosauria in the United States National Museum, with special reference to the genus Stegosaurus," *Bulletin of the United States National Museum*, 89, 1914.

Hotton, Nicholas, III, *Dinosaurs*, Pyramid Publications, New York, 1963.

Lull, Richard Swann, "A Revision of the Ceratopsia or Horned Dinosaurs," *Memoirs of the Peabody Museum of Natural History*, 3(3): New Haven, Connecticut, 1933.

——, "Triassic Life of the Connecticut Valley," revised edition, *Bulletin of the Connecticut Geological Natural History Survey*, 81, 1963.

—— and Wright, Nelda E., "Hadrosaurian Dinosaurs of North America," *Geological Sociaty of North America*, Special Papers, No. 40, Baltimore, 1942.

Marsh, Othniel Charles, "The Dinosaurs of North America," *Sixteenth Annual Report of the U. S. Geological Survey*, 1896, pp. 133-244.

Ostrom, John H., "Cranial Morphology of the Hadrosaurian Dinosaurs of North America," *Bulletin of the American Museum of Natural History*, 122, article 2, 1961.

Piveteau, Jean (Editor), *Traite de Paleontologie,* Volume 5, "Amphibians, Reptiles, Oiseaux," Macson, Paris, 1955. (Albert F. de Lapparent and Rene Lavocat wrote the section pertaining to dinosaurs.)

Romer, Alfred Sherwood, *Man and the Vertebrates,* Penguin Books, Baltimore, 1933.

——, *Vertebrate Paleontology,* third edition, The University of Chicago Press, Chicago, 1967. (Of considerable value is the compiled list of dinosaur genera.)

Steel, Rodney, "Ornithischia," *Handbuch der Paläoherpetologie* (*Encyclopedia of Paleoherpetology*), Part 15, edited by Oskar Kuhn, Gustav Fischer Verlag, Stuttgart and Portland, 1969.

Swinton, W. E., *Dinosaurs,* third edition, Trustees of the British Museum (Natural History), London, 1967.

——, *The Dinosaurs,* Wiley-Interscience, London and New York, 1968.

——, *Fossil Amphibians and Reptiles,* Trustees of the British Museum (Natural History), London, 1965.

Wendt, Herbert, *Before the Deluge,* Doubleday & Co., Garden City, New York, 1968. (Translated by Richard and Clara Winston.)

Zangerl, Rainer, *Dinosaurs, Predator and Prey,* Chicago Natural History Museum (Field Museum) Press, Chicago, March, 1956.

Zittel, Earl A. von, *Textbook of Palaeontology,* Macmillan and Co., London, 1932.